IMMIGRATION, IMMIGRATION, IMMIGRATION, AND MORE IMMIGRATION TO NO END

I0467951

Folks, over the years in my writing I have said very little on immigration, in fact I don't think I've ever written an entire article on immigration.

My views on immigration still hold that immigration is a symptom not a cause. And in my view treating symptoms is basically a waste of time and energy. I hear all kinds of conspiracy theories and other stuff on how all of these very young illegal children are flooding into the country and on and on.

But, the way I see it, the cause can be traced directly to liberalism and our welfare state. The survival of our whole system of government was never under threat before 1938 with the enacting of the socialist "Minimum wage law," which leads to what I have been Hammering and pounding to no end.

The USA is doomed, the shallow minded liberals has just about succeeded in destroying this great free nation. I love liberals, they are good Americans, it's just that they are too shallow to be trusted with total power.

Many has written me off and dismissed me as

that kook or nut that wants to repeal and get rid of the minimum wage law entirely. So be it, I will go to my grave knowing that I'm right on this.

I have supernatural wisdom and can dissect an economy as well as anyone. And I'm telling you the USA cannot be saved unless the socialist minimum wage law is repealed.

My beloved homeland the USA has already started unraveling before our eyes and there is no power on earth that can get us through this as one nation except a true free market place economy. But, it is impossible to have a true free market place economy with a socialist "Minimum wage law" in place.

The minimum wage law must be repealed now, tomorrow may be too late. Once the socialist minimum wage law is repealed the immigration problem will solve itself. With no minimum wage law the over powering suction and attraction that beckons immigrants will no longer exist.

I don't have any proof, but I'm going to go out on a limb and make a bold prediction. I predict soon some nations around the world are going to get rid of any socialist minimum wage law entirely and allow a true free market place economy to sink or swim on its own. We'll see.

Is Immigration A Blessing In Disguise?

In my humble opinion there is no such thing as guaranteed lasting wealth anymore; to me it's all a fantasy with no physical connection to reality. Wealth is supposed to represent spent energy and show a direct link to spent energy.

Whoosh, wealth here today but could be gone tomorrow, rich or poor, no one is an exception. If you think this welfare state beast won't seize all bank account to pay it's bills, just keep on living.

Ninety five percent of the population in the USA is living in fantasy land. They have no real concept of private enterprise profit and how it is the life blood of government and our entire survival. I can only express my one man opinion of the sad state of my beloved USA homeland.

I am old enough to remember when the news media and the government placed the law above all else in this great nation. Now, in my view the liberal news media itself is a threat to the survival of our great nation. I believe they are so partisan that the law means very little to them anymore. Why should anyone have total faith in the law anymore when those in high places place politics and outcome above the law?

Again, only strong discipline can save the great USA now. Only repealing the 1938 socialist minimum wage law will unshackle our phony P.... of a free market place economy, then as a reborn genuine true free market place economy it will start kicking ass and taking names and save this great country from total doom.

All of these people crowding into the USA illegally thinking they are going to have a great future may actually be coming aboard a sinking ship in my view. I'm one that is not one hundred percent for sure that the USA is going to survive as one nation unless some drastic changes are made and soon.

I'm just being honest, Unless the 1938 socialist "Minimum wage" law is repealed and gotten rid of entirely I can't see a snowball chance in hell of the USA surviving another five years as one free nation. Hell, I hope and pray that I'm wrong on this.

I understand and can dissect an economy as well as anyone. And I'm telling you the liberal's death grip hold on this country is just too great. And the only power on earth that can break that grip and save the USA is a genuine true free market place economy.

But I repeat, there is a catch, it is impossible to have a true pure free market place economy with a "Minimum wage" law in place. Either the USA repeals the 1938 "Minimum wage" law or the USA die. It's just

that simple, my intention is not to scare
anyone, but that is just the way I see it,
sorry. We'll soon see one way or another.

Plus, I got news for conservatives and
republicans, cutting spending or government
will only get you quickly booted out of office,
period. With no warning just do it, just repeal
the 1938 socialist "Minimum wage" law
entirely, and then be still.

A genuine true free market place economy
will fight your battle and save this last
bastion of true individual freedom left in the
world today. It won't be pretty but the USA
will survive as one unified free nation.

Otherwise, very soon with no official nation
language we might as well kiss a free nation
with individual freedom goodbye for another
10,000 years or maybe never to return.

I think the liberals if not provoking something
to bring about martial law will gladly seize the
least opportunity if it presents itself. The
hand writing is on the wall that is why they
fear and hate the tea party so much.

Boy, the liberals would shut down free speech
in a New York minute if they had martial law.
With all of the lying and conniving going on in
high places the liberal media knows that laws
are being broken, but, in their minds it's
them against us and to hell with placing the

law and country first.

That is why I know the only thing that can save the USA at this late stage is to repeal the 1938 minimum wage law that would bring about a true free market place economy. Only the accountability, responsibility, and discipline that come with a genuine true free market place economy can save the USA from total doom, this I swear.

The other day I seen in the news that the Brooklyn Bridge, Golden Gate Bridge and most of our great bridges and infrastructures were built before the 1938 socialist minimum wage law was enacted. Just the facts ma'am, just the facts. So, don't tell me repealing the minimum wage law won't provide jobs, jobs, jobs galore and save this great country.

Look like Benjamin Franklin was right, we had a republic but liberalism won't let us keep it. **SIRMANS LOG; 10 JUNE 2014, 1421 HOURS**

THE FINAL SOLUTION!
The struggle to survive: Man and nature has evolved over time and I'm one that believes that if you take the struggle out of survival man will destroy himself.

I think balance in all things assures the best chance of survival. Even love that is not balanced with discipline can be a very dangerous thing. Look at nature itself, with its law of survival of the strongest and the fittest, it shows no mercy, you eat or get eaten.

I believe all human emotions evolved to aid human survival in some way. I think one of the most important things in human survival is the nuclear and extended family system. And the number one reason is it provides the safest and most stable environment to teach the young norms and traditions. Otherwise, each generation will veer off down dangerous and uncharted territory.

Norms and traditions are what maintains order and keeps a society civilized. The "New deal" programs seized the provider role and took it away from the poor traditionally male head of household, but government never instilled norms and traditions in the young like before.

To me that is like a crime against survival. And we wonder why the nation is falling apart. With no norms and traditions being instilled in the young all of the knowledge and experienced passed down from generations was lost when government became a social and family provider.

The USA is now faced with a situation that no amount of knowledge and education can prevent total chaos; only raw nature can save us now. Look at the children invasion situation, it is unsolvable, we are a caring and compassionate nation.

In a way it is a blessing in disguised, now, just maybe, the USA will do what must be done if it is to survive. Only one thing can save the USA, "A raw genuine true free market place economy" And all that is necessary to get us there is to repeal the 1938 "Minimum wage" law now, tomorrow may be too late.
SIRMANS LOG: 23 JUNE 2014, 2142 HOURS

WHY ARE BOAR HOGS CASTRATED???
The term: "Conception is reality" seem to be more wide spread than anytime in history. On TV they were saying a lady rode to an election victory because of her Ad about her castrating boar hogs.

Wow! As a soon to be 72 year old, that took me all the way back to the late 1940's and early 1950's as a 9 or 10 year old living on a farm in Stockton, Georgia. Today very few young people know how our meats are raised and slaughtered.

Except for the very few our meat comes from the grocery store and that's as far as they ever knows. My family left the farm when I was 14 years old and to this day I don't know the whole story on why they castrate boar hogs before slaughter.

I think it's done to make the meat more tender with a less strong flavor, but, big deal, I'm not about to spend time researching it. Anyway! I would sit and watch as my dad and two or three other men would hold down a big boar hog and castrate him.

I don't know but I'm sure the big factory like farms of today have racks for that sort of thing. But, back then they had to manually hold down the big boar hogs which was no easy task.

Holding the hind legs of a big boar hog can be like holding two powerful jack hammer pistons, and a man can get seriously injury if not careful. Once they would get the boar stable one man would use a sharp knife and make a slit, then squeeze the mountain oyster out and cut the connecting cord, done.

Back then it was before the blow fly was eradicated. I can't remember the name of the medicine they used, all I remember is they mixed it with used motor oil. They had on hand a bucket of this medicine and motor oil mixture and used a stick with a rag wrapped around the end to apply this mixture to the wound.

Back then before the blow fly was eradicated screw worms would quickly get into a wound and do disaster like damage. So, the screw worm medicine was a must and was applied until the wound healed.

City dwellers may not know what the hell is going on here, but, you can bet your bottom dollar that there is a lot of people in this great country that still cherish old norms and traditions, including me. Glory be to God.
SIRMANS LOG: 07 JUNE 2014, 1429 HOURS

DO DUTY, HONOR, AND COUNTRY MEAN WHAT IT USE TO?
When you see all of the ado and outcry of things taking place in the USA today, there is one common thread going through it all, liberalism. And the saddest part of all about the situation is nothing is going to change.

Sure, the "Affordable Care Act" (Obamacare) by law was enacted to be in almost full affect by now, but the Dems have it in "Fool the suckers" mode until after the November election.

The Dems are hoping they can hold on to their majority in the U.S. Senate because if they do we the citizens are going to get all of Obamacare then, and dry too. And all of the terrible misery and hardship ain't going to be pretty. So, if you give someone a stick, why complain when he use it on you, people.

I hear cocky people on the TV all pumped up on believing there is going to be some big republican gain or sweep in November, yet, I'm one not totally convinced. As a self-made writer, I have pounded and pounded to no end that nothing is going to stop this liberal train to doomsday except repealing the "Minimum wage law."

I didn't just crawl out of the wood works to say something stupid. I know without a doubt what the hell I'm talking about; I can dissect an economy as well as anyone. Repealing the minimum wage law will unshackle and set the free market place free to work its magic.

There is nothing else on earth that can save the USA at this late stage; this swamp is just too infested with anti-survival negative liberalism, period. Excess business profit comes only from the private sector and is what provides practically all of the funds for the USA government to survive on.

But, due to taxes, government mandates, and government regulations fewer and fewer businesses are generating profit for government to tax. The cold steel rock hard fact is American businesses don't generate enough excess profit to support our welfare state.

Yet, Washington keeps spending and borrowing by the trillions like the USA has money to burn. Now, you are going to convince me the USA has a bright future, #@%$&*#&, I love you too. Repealing the minimum wage law will in a harmless way slowly bleed off the pressure and stop all of this madness by snuffing out inflation and providing jobs for all.

Sure, it will slowly deflate the economy and no one will earn as much money but everything you buy will drop down to where one can pay their own food and doctor bills out of pocket. But, no one hears my great supernatural wisdom to repeal the minimum wage law, I weep for the only home I know, God save my beloved homeland.
SIRMANS LOG: 05 JUNE 2014, 1429 HOURS

QUICK BASIC ECONOMIC UNDERSTANDING FOR DUMMIES
I, Freddie L sirmans, Sr. as a writer with great creative thinking ability and almost supernatural wisdom decided to make my suggestion on this VA thing. The VA is socialized medicine which has built in limitations. Still, with strong discipline, responsibility, and accountability the system could be ten times better than it is.

Now, about the economy, I feel I understand and can dissect an economy as well as anyone. So, I'm going to give a brief lecture on how an economy works as I understand it. In my view consumer inflation is something bad and dangerous, sort of like riding a tiger; the problem is staying alive when getting off.

Maybe that is why modern day economist doesn't want inflation to end. No matter what one may think an economy is made up of only two players, a seller and a buyer. Sure, it may look modern and complicated but over all an economy is very simple.

Long before a currency was invented the early economies were based on people trading and bartering with each other. But, you can't trade or barter unless you have what someone else wants. If you had a lot of potatoes and no one wanted any then you were stuck. So, as you can see some type of a currency was needed to trade for whatever one wanted.

However, with a currency also came profit, which was a God send to the growth of government. Government was now able to take directly it's cut of profit in the form of taxes or take possessions and auction them off for the profit.

Profit is generated when a seller sells a

product or service for a fee more than the cost in labor to produce the product or service. And the difference between the two is called profit. When a seller continues to sell products and services for a profit he is now a proprietor and operating what is called a business.

A business is only a medium of exchange to generate a profit, if a business fails to generate a profit it cannot exist and must close. Government itself is not part of the economy but what it does greatly influences the economy.

In a society or nation government is a must to provide internal and external protection and to do the things the people can't do for themselves. But, one thing government should never do is become a social and family provider. That is like a nation feeding on itself.

Once government becomes a social and family provider it is only a matter of time before its demand for more and more taxes become endless. Government becomes like a junkie on the streets for a tax fix until it destroys the very source of its own survival, which is the profit generated by businesses. Are we there yet? Nope, but we are getting awful close.

To finance government being a social and

family provider that money must come from a private business directly, or from the wages and possessions of it's employees. But remember, a business doesn't pay taxes, people pay taxes. A business is just a medium of exchange to generate a profit.

The working people and those who pay taxes is who pays for our welfare state. And the load has become too heavy, only our massive debt load is keeping us fed. And who knows when the bottom will drop out of that and doom us all.

In the early days of business a big problem was finding the capital to grow and expand. That problem was solved when someone came up with the idea of dividing a business into shares and selling the shares as stock. And then along comes compound interest and economics took on a life of its own.

Sure, all of this other stuff changes things, but in my view it still boils down to just two players, a seller and a buyer.

Again, I repeat, there is nothing on earth that can save the USA as a dying nation except a genuine true free market place economy. But, it is impossible to have a true free market place economy with a "Minimum wage law" in place.

For the shallow minded the "Minimum wage

law" is all about wages and a paycheck or how much one is getting paid. If the minimum wage law was repealed tomorrow I doubt there would be much sudden change in what people get paid.

There is no "Maximum wage law" on what an employer can pay for labor. To get better workers you got to pay better wages. It still holds true, you get what you pay for. My focus on the "Minimum wage law" is the mechanics of what it does to the discipline of a free market place economy at work.

Any forced wage or price control no matter how small kills the discipline in a free market place economy. All of the great production power and abundance of everything in a free market place economy is all due to its discipline. You get paid what you are worth to the business, not what the government says you are worth.

When the minimum wage law was enacted in 1938 it took the discipline out of the USA economy and our whole society has been slowly falling apart ever since. And only repealing the minimum wage law will give the USA a fighting chance of surviving the destruction of our nuclear and extended family system, our moral and spiritual values, and lack of any emergency backup bartering capacity.

Is Immigration A Blessing In Disguise?

What is called a free market place economy here in the USA today is actually a phony p.... of a true free market place economy. The USA economy of today lacks any true discipline to purge out gross inefficiency and moral decay. Discipline is what gives purpose to life.

There is no lasting success, enjoyment, or anything in life without discipline. I beg and I plead to you, bring back the discipline the USA economy once had. Repeal the 1938 discipline snatching law that forced this socialist "Minimum wage law" on needy vulnerable victims.

"Forcing" anything in a free market economy is socialist no matter what good is intended because force destroys the inherited power and discipline in a free market economy.

A "Minimum wage law" is purely a disguised socialist tool parading as something good, and surely, it fools all but the very wise. The truth of the matter is if it's so good, why force it on the people; make the "Minimum wage law" voluntarily.

Now, to shift gears, Global warming and Climate change are just liberal Hoaxes to try and take attention away from their nation destroying policies. Besides, the USA acting alone couldn't make a difference even it did matter.

The fact is "Matter" cannot be created or destroyed anyway, meaning the earth is design to constant change and adapt. Spending even one second on climate change in my view is a waste of time.
SIRMANS LOG: 30 MAY 2014, 2014 HOURS

SOME WANT A BALANCE BUDGET AMENDMENT AND CONSTITUTIONAL CONVENTION

A constitutional convention in today's climate is a dangerous and bad idea in my view. A balanced budget amendment is unneeded and a waste of time in my opinion. To me the system itself ain't broke, it's just been hijacked by the liberals.

The role of being a provider in itself calls for wielding power over others. The federal government shouldn't be a social and family provider in the first place, that is our problem in a nutshell right there. Let me say up front, I think a balance budget amendment or anything else is a waste of time for anyone thinking it is going to stop reckless spending.

As long as government is a social and family provider nothing is going to stop reckless spending until government is voted or kicked out of that role. Sure, there are many that believe a balanced budget amendment will solve the problem, but they don't truly understand human nature.

The force and drive for reckless spending is the nature of the beast, and it comes with the social and family provider territory. It is like honey to a bear, at least conservatives won't go wild, but with liberals there is no restraint when it comes to spending someone else's money.

You see, we all too some degree has become dependent to this beast, our welfare state. And as long as this beast is in the role of super social and family provider we as dependents are going to allow our leaders to beg, borrow, and even steal to keep it fed. Look at what this beast has already done to our values and morals, and we haven't seen nothing yet.

The truth is we the citizens are like little dependent children trying to demand a drunkard irresponsible parent stop reckless spending on booze, it ain't gonna happen. We the citizen gave up our independence with the "New deal" when we allowed this beast to seize the social and family provider role for itself.

Before the "New deal" seized it, for over 6,000 years the social and family provider role has always belonged to the nuclear and extended family head of household, who dutifully instilled self-restraint, respect for authority, and respect for norms and traditions in the very young.

This must be done to safeguard the future and future generations, but, when the federal government seized the provider role for itself it failed to carry out these duties. That is why our norms, morals, and values has gone to hell, and we are going to loose this great country unless the minimum wage law is repealed entirely. That will give the free market place back it's power to save this great nation, nothing else can do it.

The basic personality of an individual is shaped by the age of ten. That includes self-restraint, a respect for authority, morals, values, and society norms. So, if no one is instilling proper norms in the very young, how in the hell can anyone expect the USA to stay civilized and crime free.

There is a survival reason why norms and traditions are so important. It is like everything in life, there is no substitute for experience. Having norms and traditions safeguard us from doing a lot of dangerous and stupid stuff that leads to disaster.

The young has always thought they knew all of the answers and older folks were behind the times and didn't know what was going on. Not realizing that their parents had passed that stage years ago and certain things never change.

The young is 100 percent of our future. Liberal policy starting with government seizing the social and family provider role and making our economy impotent by adding a minimum wage law is destroying the USA from within. I beg and plead, please repeal the minimum wage law now, tomorrow may be too late.

The states did something even more stupid than the people giving up their independence, the states gave up their power to control this welfare state beast. Before the seventeenth amendment the two state senators in Washington were appointed and worked for and reported to their Governor and state legislature. They served their states self-interest, not all of these extreme environmental and other liberal groups.

The federal government's role is to collect taxes, protect the nation internally and externally, and do only the few things the people can't do for themselves, period. When the federal government becomes a social and family provider it starts feeding on itself and cannot possible survive over four or five generations in that role.

People I'm telling you our time is up with having a provider government, everything is already up-side-down. So, I'm telling you until the federal government is either voted out or kicked out of its social and family provider role no constitutional convention or balance budget amendment is going to stop reckless spending.

In our current climate it seems obvious that the federal government will never be voted out of its social and family provider role. That means the only way the USA is going to be saved from total doom is for government to be kicked out of the provider role. I'm crazy enough to believe that will soon be done.

In a free nation there is no force greater than a true genuine free market place economy, not even the law. A true free market place economy has the power to break this doomsday grip the welfare state has on this nation and give the power back to the people. But, let me add, it is impossible to have a true genuine free market place economy with any amount of a minimum wage in place.

A minimum wage law de-nuts or castrates a true free market place economy and makes it practically useless discipline-wise. And what the USA have now is not a true free market place economy, but a phony powerless effeminate punk of an economy that is about to self-destruct.

Only repealing the minimum wage law will

take the shackles off and allow a genuine true free market place economy to rise up out of the ashes like phoenix and save our dying nation. So, here is the priority of what it is going to take to save the USA from total doom.

Repeal the minimum wage law entirely, its just that simple, repeal and the USA survives, continue on as is and it will soon be over. **SIRMANS LOG: 21 MAY 2014, 1626 HOURS**

POLITICAL POLLING OUGHT TO BE OUTLAWED OR AT LEAST BANNED 3 MONTHS BEFORE MAJOR ELECTIONS. I shouldn't even be writing this article because I have already wore out the subject of talking about the minimum wage. "You can't get blood out of a turnip." Yet, demanding that businesses that are barely surviving raise wages is trying to do just that.

It says a lot, we as a nation has just about lost the knowledge of what it means to be a free people. Liberal policy has almost destroyed our sense of self-determination to somehow make it on our own ability.

I will say it again louder; our USA swamp is just too big and too crowded in liberal thinking, liberal beliefs, and shallow liberal judgment. And this nation can't possibly survive very much longer unless this swamp is drained by repealing the minimum wage law.

Ninety five percent of the American population has fell prey to this cock and bull lie that our super sugar daddy welfare state provider will always be there to take care of us from cradle to grave. No one thought like that before the "New deal seized the provider role from the nuclear family head of household.

Two liberal policies must be undone before this great country can be saved from total liberal destruction. And we are way pass the stage of no return, first the minimum wage law must be repealed or else the USA economy will soon fall into total chaos.

Sure, I totally agree with these good decent people that a person ought to be able to earn a livable wage. But, most of these people have never run a business and doesn't have a clue as to why they shouldn't be paid more. However, I excuse these people, but I don't excuse America's leaders and the news media.

True, the liberals did hijack the country with the "New deal." Still, the duty in a republic form of government is for leaders to educate the public and bring them along on what is in the best interest of the country.

It is not to circumvent the founding father's intent by insane political polling to pander to an uninformed general public. Political polling ought to be outlawed or at the very least banned three months before every major election, period.

There was a time in the USA when a woman could walk through a poor or middle class neighborhood at midnight with a purse and no one would harm her.

Yes, that was before 1938 when "New deal" liberal policy seized the social and family provider role from our nuclear and extended family system. And the final coup de grace was the enacting of the "Minimum wage law."

It is taking around eighty years for the final death rattle. But, it is similar to a poisonous snake biting a rat, the snake doesn't get in a hurry chase, it knows the rat won't get too far. It is the same with our minimum wage law; the USA economy cannot and will not survive very much longer, unless the minimum wage law is repealed, period.

PS: The fact is repealing the "Minimum wage law" will enable the American people to make a livable wage, but it is so sad that I am one of the very few with the wisdom and depth to

see it. God, I ask in your name, save my beloved homeland.
SIRMANS LOG: 16 MAY 2014, 0049 HOURS

I BELIEVE IT'S TIME FOR MEDICAL SUPERVISED FLOGGING TO BE TRIED

I believe societal-wise four or five hard lick on the rear will do more to reduce crime than ten years in modern day prison. That would be especially true with the young and first time offenders. And the big advantage is its practically free with no housing and caretaking cost to the tax payers.

Flogging is nothing new and it works. There is a lack of real discipline in the early raising in most homes today. That lack of discipline is a failure to instill self-restraint which makes one aware of consequences. I think it is time the whole USA criminal justice system considers experimenting with flogging seriously.

The prisons nationwide are already filled to the brim. Daily as I listen to the local news there is smash and grab, break-ins, muggings, and crime, crime galore. Hell, I know I'm barking up the wrong tree, because oh no, we are too civilized to stoop to something so primitive as flogging.

I'm just saying we are being over run by

crime and taking care of all these law breakers are just too expensive. I'm not talking about the sadistic cold hearted murders and rapist; of course they must be kept locked away. Folks, I'm a writer and I call a spade a spade and tell it as I see it.

It is not going to get any better folks, either we control crime or it's going to control us. **SIRMANS LOG: 08 MAY 2014, 2239 HOURS**

ECONOMICALLY IGNORANT SUCKERS, I'M TRYING TO EDUCATE YOU!
The minimum wage debate is a main reason why the founding fathers made the USA a republic form of government. Ninety five percent of the American people are in favor of raising the minimum wage.

I believe there should never have been a forced minimum wage law in the first place. And the only way to save the USA from total destruction is to repeal the minimum wage law we have now entirely. The ninety five percent supporters see the minimum wage only in terms of making more money at work, and a few see it in terms of costing jobs.

However, as a deep great thinker, in my view that hardly touches the surface as to the effect of a minimum wage law. The "Minimum wage law" of 1938 was one of the last "New deal" programs put in place.

Next to the government seizing the family provider role for itself I think forcing a minimum wage law on a free market place economy is the most dumb and destructive thing there is. Sure, the effect is not instantly but it is a poison pill like cancer that slowly eats away the inner fabric of a nation until there is nothing is left.

Look at the USA today we are practically just a shell. Our culture has been ripped to threads, our morals and spiritual values are up-side-down, and we have almost no emergency fall back bartering capacity in case our currency collapses. And the really sad, sad part is ninety five percent of the population thinks I'm stupid or some kind of nut case.

That's a judgment call, and having a minimum wage law in the first place have damaged our judgment like almost everything else. A true free market place economy has never failed to produce an over abundance of jobs, food, or what ever is needed.

But, the powers that be has never liked a true free market place economy simply because if you don't produce you don't survive no matter who you know or b... And the real secret to the success of a free market place even though few realize it is its discipline.

Authoritarian type governments keep moral and culture rot from getting out of control by brute force, but, in a free nation the only way to keep moral decay and culture rot from getting out of control is through a highly disciplined true free market place. Free countries think they are too civilized to flog law breakers or give other harsh death sentences.

I will end by saying: Enacting a minimum wage law takes the discipline out of a free market place economy, thereby giving a free country a death sentence. We are now reaping the harvest planted from the "New deal" seeds. I rest my case.

SIRMANS LOG: 02 MAY 2014, 1540 HOURS

THIS MINIMUM WAGE THING MAKE IT LOOK LIKE THE MAYANS MAY NOT BE TOO FAR OFF THE MARK AFTER ALL

The reason why 95 percent of the USA population can't understand the destruction of our minimum wage law is due to a lack of perspective. The thing about economics is you can never understand it looking at it piece meal.

It must be viewed in the whole which

includes culture, morals, spiritual, trade, and the use of a currency. Who wouldn't like to make more money, I certainly would (I heard that!). But, in economic terms just by the stroke of a pen forcing any wage control or a raise in wage control on a free market place economy means its total destruction.

No, its not instant death, but the die has been cask and about four generations into the future sun set will be almost impossible to avoid. Now, our time is up. we have had our four generations and our inner fabric have been ripped to threads.

The cancer has for all practically purpose destroyed our culture, our morals, our spiritual values, and any emergency bartering capacity to survive on. In fact we are left with just a shell with all of our inner fabric eaten away or destroyed.

And, the really, really sad part is 95 percent of the USA population has become too dependent minded and shallow to realize it. Lord have mercy. And even worse the last and only thing that could give the USA a fighting chance of survival is totally ignored, sad, sad, sad.

Abolishing the minimum wage law entirely is our last and only chance of surviving as a free nation; yet, economically ignorant people are going to raise the minimum wage control lever even higher which will speed up even the little time we have left.

I'm at my wits end, more and more it looks like the Mayans may not have been too far off the mark after all. Mans actions always determines his future. However, it's never too late to do the wise thing.
SIRMANS LOG: 25 APRIL 2014, 1249 HOURS

LATE ENTRY:
There is a reason why I chose repealing and getting rid of the minimum wage law entirely as top priority to save the USA from total doom. You see, the USA is now a swamp totally infested with all kinds of negative anti-survival swamp things.

It's just too much in here, so, the best and wisest thing is to just drain the entire USA swamp. Out of hundreds of negative anti-survival forces that can take down this great nation I'm going to name three or four.

These forces are a threat to long term survival because we may no longer be able to produce a big enough future generation to carry on.

Example: We already have mass use of birth control pills, mass use of abortions on demand, and thanks to the courts we now have mass use of men marring men and women marring women. What else is new?

Now, you are going to convince me that there is no long term threat to this great nation, #@&%*#$@, I love you too. That was only a sample of what growing more powerful everyday in this swamp.

Repealing the minimum wage law in one sweep nationwide will in a harmless controlled manner drain this swamp. This will kill two birds with one stone, by starving the welfare beast out of power and setting the free market place free at last to save us all.

And as a bonus the provider power will revert back to the nuclear family and the people where it has always been until the "New deal" seized it.

SIRMANS LOG: 26 APRIL 2014, 1940 HOURS

CONSERVATIVES VERSUS OBAMACARE
Never mind trying to fix Obamacare or anything else concerning it. My advice to conservatives is get the hell away from the ball. The liberals are behind late in the fourth with little time remaining and punting out of their own inzone.

To conservatives never mind a fair catch or running it back, just get the hell away from the ball. And don't try anything fancy just go ahead and run out the clock with things that has been proven to work for conservatives.

To hell with the pollsters or how boring it becomes, just stay with lower taxes, more jobs, and strong national defense. And for God sake stay away from details until after the election no matter how much the liberal press pisses and moans.

Otherwise, the liberal press as always will paint conservatives as mean and uncaring, which always highly influences our gullible electorate. That only worked in the past because of pseudo conservative tactics and being all over the map.

Stay with your proven strong running game, it wins championships.
SIRMANS LOG: 22 APRIL 2014, 1344 HOURS

PS: My advice, stay away from Obamacare. In my view it stinks, it smells, and is just one big gutter insurance mess. And you know what they say about the gutter, if you crawl down in the gutter for a fight, no one comes out smelling like a rose. Stay the hell away from it; let it rot away on its own.

Conservatives must anchor down with lower taxes and more jobs without details instead of going all over the map on side issues. That's because for the next two years the liberals are going to keep some kind of racial or extreme side issue going to turnout their main base.

Conservatives can't lose if they pound over and over like mad men/women, more jobs and lower taxes. That will build base trust instead of selling ones soul for a vote they'll never get. Even many liberals will vote for someone they trust and believe will actually fight tooth and nails for more jobs and lower taxes.

The real problem with the Republican Party is they don't trust the American people and the people don't trust them in return. Why should the people trust the Republicans because in the last presidential election they ran from the words "Lower taxes" like it was the plague? When Republicans no longer fight for lower taxes they don't deserve to win in my view.

Like it or not, pollsters or not, if the Republicans ever expect to win the big one again, the people must believe without a doubt that they will fight tooth and nails for more jobs and lower taxes. The people already know without a doubt that the Dems are going to fight tooth and nails for bigger government and higher taxes.

If you want to throw caution to the wind and live in the moment, then go ahead and join

the Dems, as for me, I will go down trying to do what I can to help save my country from insane spending.
SIRMANS LOG: 23 APRIL 2014, 1640 HOURS

SICK AND TIRED OF BEING SICK AND TIRED

I get so sick and tired of sheer economic ignorant people thinking raising the minimum wage is going to help this economy. In fact the only thing that is going to save this economy from total doom is out right repealing and getting rid of the minimum wage or any wage control entirely.

Since 1938 the minimum wage law has allowed the liberals to get control of the USA economy which is a little over four generations. Like I have said many times you can get almost any cock-eyed economic system to work for four or five generations, then its sun set time.

Sure, the intention was to do good, but, economic-wise installing a minimum wage or any kind of wage or price control on a free market place economy is dumb, stupid, and destructive, period. It is a dagger right into the heart of a free market place economy and it ignites inflation, then after four generation it is impossible to keep inflation from spinning out of control.

Is Immigration A Blessing In Disguise?

I'm going to say it even if the egg heads and Keynesian economist never will. Raising the minimum wage just may be the straw that breaks the camels back and sends what's left of the wobbly-kneed USA economy over the cliff.

I'm just sick and tired of people who should know better keeping the people economically ignorant just to go along to get along. We need leaders calling a spade a spade. And I'm telling you the only way to improve the lives of the people and save the USA economy is to set the free market place free, not cripple and weigh it down even more with a higher wage control.

I'm just tired of the economic ignorance of it all to see my beloved homeland go down the tube with liberal policy. And to this day they are still lying and fooling the people with pie in the sky for all. Don't get it twisted, I love liberals, they bring happiness and make the world a far better place, who else will make sure Bambi is always safe and protected.

It's just that liberals should never have total power because most lack depth and live in the moment in my view. However, there is nothing innate about being a liberal, many has been converted to a conservative over night when a mugger slammer one upside the head or burglarized one's home.

Being a liberal is mostly a lack of survival awareness more than anything else. Discipline is what makes one more aware of what's a threat to survival and it instills in one what is call a survival instinct. And one with a strong survival instinct automatically knows and feels what is a threat to survival including the unborn, too.

That is why those with strong survival instinct just knows and feels without being told that certain things are a threat to survival. However, since the government kicked the poor black man out of the home and failed to instill discipline itself most young black males lack self-restraint and has very weak survival instincts. This government act has all but totally destroyed the black community and is fast engulfing the entire nation.

In no way am I putting down most young black males, in fact under the circumstance most are overcoming great odd and turning out well and successful. And in the big liberal controlled inner cities that's totally gang infested the odd are stacked overwhelmingly against most young black males, yet many still escape to Morehouse and other great institutions.

Many black women complain about black men in general, and my answer is always the same as a question. Who do you think shaped and molded the values of most black men today? You know the answer to that.

Excuse me folks, I just got carried away; I just had to vent; now I feel better. Still, the minimum wage law must be repealed and gotten rid of entirely, now, tomorrow may be too late.
SIRMANS LOG: 19 APRIL 2014, 1211 HOURS

TO SEE OR NOT TO SEE, HALLELUJAH!
Who are you going to believe, me or your lying eyes? A wise man knows there are times when you should cut your losses and move on. The USA is the only home I know and I feel duty bound to do what I can for the survival of my homeland.

I know the repeal of the minimum wage law is the only thing that can save my country. You can lead a horse to water, but you can't make him drink. It's the same when I plead and I plead, please repeal and get rid of the minimum wage law entirely.

I'm at my wits end; you can't make a man see something right before his eyes until he wakes up. There has been countless cases where people have suffered bad accidents or other dreadful things, yet, said they were glad it happened.

They said things right before their eyes they could never see before they can now see very clearly. You can call me a nut, kook, or whatever you like, but I can see clearly things right before our eyes most people will never be able to see.

That is because I have paid a severe mental price through a life long mental battle and struggle. Yet, I have no monopoly on pain, struggle, or suffering, I'm just thankful to have my life health and strength, Hallelujah. **SIRMANS LOG: 17 APRIL 2014, 2103 HOURS**

THE USA VOTERS STILL HAS THE POWER TO DE-CLAW OUR WELFARE STATE BEAST
Okay, ignorance is ignorance no matter how you look at it. And that is what has happen to the USA since the government seized the social and family provider role from the nuclear family unit. There is a world of difference between learned intelligence and wisdom.

To set up a system of government like we had before the "New deal," it took men of great wisdom. In fact, almost everyone of that era had good wisdom and strong survival instincts due only to just the struggle of day to day living.

Is Immigration A Blessing In Disguise?

Today most independent minded people in the USA know we are in trouble and can't survive with the way our welfare state beast is out of control. But, they don't have a clue as to the real answer, they just want their freedom and rights back.

The American people still have the voting power to reset this country back on course but don't have the wisdom or survival instinct to see what is right in front of their eyes. I'll lay it out, there are two main things that happen around four generations ago that brought this country to the condition it's in today.

Sure, during the great depression the very poor and handicapped needed government help. But, government should never have become a social and family provider handing out free money on an individual basis.

(1.) Once that mistake was made the system destruction die was cast. And until that deadly mistake is corrected and the nuclear family unit is restored to power the USA cannot and will not survive. That was the birth of our welfare state which has practically destroyed our economy, our culture, and our moral and spiritual values.

Men are marring men and women are marring women, all while mass murder is taking place within the womb. And 90 percent of the USA population accepts this as normal, what am I missing here, is it too late for the USA.

(2.) In 1938 the last of the "New deal" programs was put in place, the "Minimum wage law." That act was a dagger in the heart of a true free market place economy; it awakened the sleeping monster called inflation. Otherwise, a true free floating free market place with no controls is like a liquid, it will always find its own level.

But, not any more, inflation and the U.S. economy is now like a car with no reverse or a hot water heater with no pop off valve, that is what the minimum wage law has done to this once great USA economy. So, I will advise anyone thinking about saving the USA, until these two boogie men is caged and sent packing that is an impossible task.

You can go to a flat tax or enact any law; our welfare state beast will laugh at you, smile, and then go spend another trillion in debt. But, repealing the minimum wage law to this beast is like the iron cross or the silver bullet riding in on a white horse as destiny to save the greatest nation to ever exist.
SIRMANS LOG: 15 APRIL 2014, 1449 HOURS

WHO TRUMPS, A TRUSTFUL AND

RESPONSIBLE CONSERVATIVE OR A BIG GOVERNMENT LIBERAL?

The hand writing is on the wall that liberals are on their way out of power. To conservatives, never count your chicks before they hatch. There is a reason why liberals has taken over and dominates news, education, and nearly every institution in America.

These extremely intelligent super aggressive shallow minded people will not let anything stop them from getting and keeping power. If conservatives think these people are going to lose power without pulling out all of the stops they may be in for a rude awakening. No matter how advantageous the Obamacare nightmare may look it is still not a done deal to defeat the Dems.

Here is why, approaching half of the voting population has a dependent mentality like a child to his mother in favor of the Dems. In that group are the African Americans we know is going to vote 95 percent in favor of the Dems. And the females to a lesser degree we know are going vote a big majority in favor of the dems.

Plus, the predominately liberal news media we know is going to focus on and praise every extreme liberal side issue. And on the other hand we know the mass media is going to demonize almost everything the conservative's tries to advance. There, you

Is Immigration A Blessing In Disguise?

see for yourself where the advantages lie.

Myself, I am an independent, but with conservative leaning. I think listening to the pollsters is the reason the republicans has lost the last three presidential elections. Things like faith and trust may not show up in polls. No one beats the liberals at their own game.

Everyone knows the Dems are going to hand out goodies and tax and spend to kingdom come. And everyone knows that republicans once were for lower taxes, more jobs, and strong national defense. But, not any more, no one knows what the republicans stand for now, except trying to out pander the Dems...

I'm sure that is the main reason the republicans lost the last three presidential elections. So, my advice to the Republicans: Obamacare alone can't be depended on to defeat the Dems, because everything including the kitchen sink is going to be thrown at republicans.

Forget about trying to out pander the Dems, besides, no one will believe and trust you anyway. Just lock on like a pit bull to only three or four proven winners such as, lower taxes, more jobs, and strong nation defense.

When elections can't be won with these three things, it won't really matter because that means freedom is lost forever in America. Just stay with three or four proven winners, otherwise being all over the map allows the liberal media to rip you to threads.

I believe there is still a majority of independent minded American voters that will choose someone they truly believe will lower taxes, provide jobs, and keep our country strong over a big government candy-man.

All the republicans need to do is stand for lower taxes, more jobs, and strong nation defense. And stay the hell away from details because that is a fools game the liberals will try to trap you in to no end.

But, in order for the republicans to be trusted as a political party ever again it must be trusted without a doubt to stand firmly for at least one or two things come hell or high waters.

Everybody knows without a doubt that the Dems stands for goodies and freebies, and taxing and spending. So, forget about trying to out give the Dems because they will gladly give away the store and the country too to stay in power. You are not going to out give um or out spend um, ever.
SIRMANS LOG: 12 APRIL 2014, 2240 HOURS

IT IS IMPOSSIBLE TO SAVE USA ECONOMY AS LONG AS GOVERNMENT IS A SOCIAL AND FAMILY PROVIDER, PERIOD.
People that don't understand economics or how the free market place actually work automatically think getting rid of the minimum wage is dumb and stupid and will increase our hardship, wrong.

In fact it is just the opposite in reality. Sure, given time one won't make as much money, but, it will bring earnings and the cost of living back in balance. And $5.00 will buy a weeks worth of grocery.

I must have said it a thousand times. Unless the government is voted out or kicked out of its social and family provider role somehow there is just no way the USA can survive very much longer.

I hear people on the air talking all the time about every way one can imaging on what will save America. Again, I repeat a thousand and one times, it is impossible to save the USA as long as government is a social and family provider.

Government as a social and family provider is like incest, it is a system that feeds on itself. Sure, almost any economic system can last four or five generations then its lights out. What happens then is it can't get around a law of nature.

Sooner or later everything that exists must
go through a life or death, or boom or bust
cycle. The minimum wage law won't let the
economy carry out a natural boom and bust
cycle. Therefore the negative anti-survival
forces have grown too powerful in the USA.

Now the USA is in a position where moral
decay and culture rot is going to take us out
if a collapsing economy doesn't get to us first.
The way I see it to save the USA it will take a
two step process.

The main focus is the government must
abandon or be voter out of its social and
family provider role or all is lost. But, that
ain't gonna happen. So, by repealing the
minimum wage law that should kill two birds
with one stone, kick the government out of
the family provider role and save the country
too.

The power must be restored back to the
people. It belongs back to the strong nuclear
and extended family unit where it has always
been for over 6,000 years until the "New
Deal" came along. Repealing the minimum
wage law will bring about a controlled orderly
rebirth that will save our nation.

Otherwise, its no longer a matter of our
welfare state collapsing, it is a matter of how

many months, or even day we have left. I
know I stand almost alone on knowing only
repealing the minimum wage law can save
us.

I beg and I plead to my fellow man/woman to
demand we repeal the minimum wage law. If
you disagree with me on repealing this law,
God bless you, almost everyone else does,
too. Still, someway some how it will be
repealed, it must.
**SIRMANS LOG: 03 APRIL 2014, 1934
HOURS**

**THEM MEAN OLD EVIL REPUBLICANS
AND CONSERVATIVES!**
Almost everyone is in an uproar about the
USA government giving up control of the
Internet. However, I believe hardcore liberal
lions and lionesses want the U.S. to give up
control of the Internet. And they want it bad.

I think they view talk radio and conservative
Internet as a big threat to their domination
and that will be a first step on silencing these
blabber mouths. They don't know how yet,
but I believe they believe that will be a foot in
the door.

So, in my view these people will do almost
anything if it will stop them mean old evil
Republicans and conservatives from telling on
them.

SIRMANS LOG: 31 MARCH 2014, 2258 HOURS

GREAT THINKER FREDDIE L SIRMANS SR. GIVES HIS VIEWS ON THE SURVIVAL OF THE USA ECONOMY
Folks, I decided to do a little brain storming on the state of USA survival. We are in it now, but, I will say it again this idea of a global economy is a fool's game in my opinion. It will never work unless one country had total domination, and that ain't gonna happen.

These globalists have come up with the North American Free Trade Agreement (NAFTA) and a host of other job sellouts in my view. Now it is water over the dam, saving the country is top priority now. I blame liberals for the dire condition the USA is in today, but, what good is that going to do, none.

Overall the "New deal" programs were intended to do good and help the people have a better life. However, human nature is what it is. Power corrupts and absolute power corrupts absolutely. No one political party alone has brought the USA to the dire situation it is in today.

It is not about right or wrong or getting righteous people in place, it is about getting people elected that have the common sense to do what have been proven to work. In other words it is the system in place that really matters. And that is the unforgivable sin I blame on the "New deal" programs they destroyed the system the founding fathers left in place.

Now, we have a corrupted and run-a-way system that allows lying, twisting of the law, and all kinds of anti-survival things to strive. Here are the two main things that brought about our run-a-way economy. Number one, the new deal programs seized the family provider role for itself and failed to carry out the discipline and responsibility of being a provider.

That act caused our culture to deteriorate with each succeeding generation, now in the home if it feels good do it. Plus, once government becomes a family provider, economically it starts feeding on itself and eating its seed corn. It takes around four generations to totally self destruct but by then the culture and all the inner fabric of the country is gone and there is nothing to rebuild on.

Right now, every thing else aside, the only way I see the USA having any chance of surviving is to repeal the minimum wage law, and that will only give us a fighting chance. The number two thing is what gives fuel to our run-a-way economy.

Is Immigration A Blessing In Disguise?

In 1938 the "New deal" programs enacted the "Minimum wage law" that removed all free market place dampers and allowed government to then tax and spend to no end. In other words with a minimum wage law in place there is no way to balance the cost of living to earnings. End result is fewer and fewer working to take care of more and more not working.

That process destroys the culture, the nuclear family, small farmers, and home gardeners, and then when it all collapses we have no foundation to rebuild upon. I will now touch on today's political situation. Due to Obamacare it looks like the Republicans may take total control of congress in November 2014.

If the liberals hadn't destroyed our true free market place system I believe the USA could have out lasted the Roman Empire but I'm afraid unless a miracle happens we are done. The Roman Empire lasted a thousand years. The Republicans think they can cut spending and save our out of control run-a-way economy, wrong.

I will say it again; the USA and Western Europe welfare states cannot be saved. Cutting spending piece meal here and there will only make the economy worse. It will also piss off half or more of the people. That will only guarantee the shallow minded liberals will be voted right back in control. Yet, cutting spending is the course the Republicans are locked on.

For the most part liberals mean well and want to care for everyone, it's just that human being are not just cogs in some big machine. Humans being are motivated by reward and punishment and responds accordingly. But, most liberals are too shallow to understand that, still, I love them and they are good Americans.

If the government was kicked out of it social and family provider role that would solve our run-a-way out of control spending problem, but that ain't gonna happen. So, here are the cold steel rock hard facts, if the USA is ever going to be saved only conservative have the will and sense to do it.

I think the anti-survival opposition has grown so powerful that the conservatives have time for just one shot at our survival target. And if the target is missed the anti-survival death grip will never be broken and that means sunset for the USA. The target I'm referring to is repealing the minimum wage law.

Conservatives need to tread water and hold off on any major spending cuts until after 2016. Then after 2016 repeal the minimum wage law once and for all. Repealing the minimum wage law won't be any peace meal deal, it will deal with the entire USA economy nation wide in one sweep.

That will allow the poor and middle class to pay out of pocket for their own food and medical bills. And it will mean jobs, jobs galore for all nationwide. Sure, one won't make as much money but the lower cost of living won't require one to need as much money.

However, I believe this but the problem is very few conservatives agree with me on anything. Like it or not there is no other way for the USA to survive.

As for the very, very poor and needy the government will need to establish government run commissaries, housing, and clinics for them. And use tokens or scrip for all who qualify.

God, I ask in your name save my homeland, the USA.
SIRMANS LOG: 29 MARCH 2014, 1852 HOURS

CONCERNING TRAIN OPERATORS AND OTHER WORKERS ON MUST STAY AWAKE JOBS:
There is a no cost very low tech technique to prevent one from falling asleep. It cannot not

be used in every situation, but will certainly work where there is a hard flat floor. I have personally used this technique many times on a must stay awake job.

Many years ago when I worked as a Federal Firefighter sometimes in the middle of the night we would have to standby on welding's or other situations. Just sitting there most of the time no problem, but a few times I did use this low tech technique to make sure I stay awake.

This is how the technique works, just hold in your hand car keys or any small object and if you start to doze it will drop to the floor with a loud enough sound to snap you back alert. First rule, immediately pick the item back up.

Here is a little brain storming to inventors: Come up with something to hold in one hand that will emit a signal every time it is dropped.
SIRMANS LOG: 26 MARCH 2014, 2011 HOURS

NOTE OF FACT:
As I have said before, being $17,000,000,000,000,000,000 in debt means the USA will soon be sold off piece meal to foreigners. Otherwise, eventually the USA will be taken over without even a shot being fired

unless the minimum wage law is repealed.

This giving away control of the internet is proof enough of my dire predictions. I believe if you scratch deep enough our national debt has compromised the USA in some way. The minimum wage law has all but destroyed our culture and it must be repealed before nothing is left.

Culture wise the USA is fast approaching the point of no return where there is not enough people left with the judgment or common sense to remain a free people. I plead for my mother land, repeal the minimum wage law before it is too late.

SIRMANS LOG: 15 MARCH 2014, 2101 HOURS

ONLY A TRUE FREE MARKET PLACE ECONOMY CAN SAVE THE USA.

There is no substitute for experience no matter what it is in life. There is an old saying that youth is wasted on the young. Experience is one of the most valued things in life, yet, economy-wise it is totally ignored.

Another old saying: When everything else fails, read the directions. Look at our economic problems, we are in no mans land, uncharted territory, or some other metaphor, yet we ignore what has been proven to always work, a true free market place.

The reason we ignore over 5,000 years of proven experience on a system that has never fails is because we as human beings are controlled by logic and self-interest. That is why I know without a doubt that it is impossible to save the USA economy unless the minimum wage law is repealed.

The USA can go to a flat tax or any other kind of tax system, or enact any law, but nothing is going to stop government from taxing and spending the USA out of existence except repealing the minimum wage law. It's simple, once government seized the provider role for itself there is no peaceful way out without facing the pitchforks.

Besides, once the government tasted the god like power of being a super provider, they got drunk on it and will never voluntarily give up an inch of that power.

SIRMANS LOG: 14 MARCH 2014, 2249 HOURS

THE SEEMINGLY IMPOSSIBLE OUT OF THE TWILIGHT ZONE "VP" WORDS MAY ACTUALLY BE IN PLAY.
This is something so remote and unthinkable as to be out of the twilight zone. The "VP" words could actually be in play.

I'm no history buff, but the "VP" words are so remote that I don't think they have ever happen from one party since the birth of the nation in 1776.

It is a well known fact that the republicans want to get rid of Obamacare and start from scratch. That being the case the unthinkable or seemingly impossible in the November 2014 election could possible happen.

A "Veto Proof" congress to get rid of Obamacare once and for all is no longer something out of "The twilight zone." That is just how bad this whole colossal socialist Obamacare boondoggle could become.
SIRMANS LOG: 13 MARCH 2014, 2233 HOURS

WHY THE MINIMUM WAGE MUST BE REPEALED IF INDIVIDUAL FREEDOM IS TO SURVIVE!
Very few people have the wisdom to see it, but the reason I drumbeat so hard on repealing the minimum wage law is: It will kick big government out of its seized social and family provider role and return that role back to the nuclear family where it has been for over 5,000 years.

Rebuilding the strong nuclear and extended family system is the only thing that is going to prevent the USA and western civilization from collapsing back to the Stone Age. The whole welfare state foundation revolves around the minimum wage law being in place, otherwise, a true free market place economy wouldn't allow all of this inflating and printing of worthless money.

The reason why a true free market place economy with unrestricted competition never fails is because of its strong discipline. And the key ingredients for that discipline are letting the market place determine free floating labor and price levels. So, when government set any price or labor level in a free market economy it distorts the process and sends discipline out the window.

When the "New deal" programs seized the social and family provider role from the nuclear family provider that was bad enough, but the slow death pill for individual freedom was the enacting of the 1938 minimum wage law. Now, there is nothing that can stop our big government beast from taxing and spending this nation out of existence except the repealing of the minimum wage law.

Even that may not save us but it is the only thing that will give us a fighting chance to survive, because all of our survival tools such as a strong nuclear and extended family system, strong moral and spiritual values, and adequate small farmers and home gardeners for bartering capacity when money is worthless are almost nonexistence.

Anyone with an ounce of economic understanding knows the USA economy is going to totally collapse or the country will be sold off piece meal to foreigners, the powers that be will never tell you that, but I just did.

I'm fixing to say something that if I had any sense I would never utter a word on the subject, but so be it. Here goes, I and a lot of people wonder where my great supernatural wisdom comes from. I never went past high school and have never read any books on economics or very little on anything else.

Now, to destroy any credibility I have left if I ever had any in the first place. This is where I suspect my great wisdom comes from: Brace yourself, I believe in reincarnation and suspect I was a German or Austrian scientist in a past life. So, how do you like me now?

PS: Remember, I write what I believe, and believe what I write. However, occasionally I may throw in something solely for shock value. In this case, you decide, if I'm for-real.

SIRMANS LOG: 08 MARCH 2014, 1015 HOURS

I'M CURSED WITH THIS GREAT WISDOM,

AND WONDER, WHY, WHY ME OH LORD, AND AGAIN, WHY NOT ME!
I know beyond a shadow of doubt that government as a social and family provider has all but totally destroyed the USA, yet I am so alone on realizing that fact. We have been fortunate to survive this long with government playing that role, but the price to the nation has taken an awesome toll.

It has all but totally destroyed our culture, our moral and spiritual values, and any adequate emergency bartering capacity with small farmers and home gardeners in case the economy collapses. We have almost no small farmer and home gardeners like what got this nation through the Great depression.

We have no means of surviving except back to the Stone Age. Government as a social and family provider for all practical purpose has all but totally sucked the life blood out of this once great independent nation. I write, I preach, and I plead to deaf ears over and over on what will save this great nation, all to no avail.

But why, oh Lord why, why won't someone listen when I plead that repealing the minimum wage law will save this great nation by freeing the people to save themselves and the government, too. What good is a raise in the minimum wage when it's just more money for government to take, waste, and squander away. Plus, it will definitely driver up the cost of everything we buy even higher.

After the minimum wage is raised and you sum it up the cost of living will be ratcheted up another notch, which will be a net loss to the poor and middle class, duh. Sure, back before we had a minimum wage law people made far less money, but, $5.00 would buy nearly twenty times what it will today.

If you was lucky enough to make it to middle class you could afford a saving account and didn't have to live from pay check to pay check. Again, we must repeal the minimum wage law or we die. It is sheer ignorance not to realize the minimum wage law must be repeal. The roads, bridges, sewage system, and infrastructure all over the country is falling apart and only repealing the minimum wage law can we get it done, duh.

The liberals seized the social and family provider role from the traditional nuclear family head of household in the "New deal" era. It is impossible for government to survive very long as a provider to the people because every penny the government gets is taken from the earnings of the people in the first place.

Governments sole role in a free society is to take only enough tax money from the people to provide internal and external (military) security for the nation. And to take care of the interior and do only the things the people can't do for themselves, period. Government as a provider is like eating your seed corn and drinking your priming water, sheer ignorance.

Just the day to day survival in days of old taught most people this simple basic wisdom. Back then nature and the elements were relentless and unforgiving. If you failed to teach your young responsibility and accountability you may not have any left.

This great wisdom I have is a curse to me because I see so clearly what must be done, yet, my beloved mother land marches on and on to sure doom. I plead and I beg do what must be done to survive, repeal the minimum wage law before it is too late.
SIRMANS LOG: 04 MARCH 2014, 1554 HOURS

DUMB, DUMB, AND DUMBER!
Folks, I'm a self-made writer and sometimes I wonder why I keep writing. I do comment on something's I have no business butting in on. But, thank God I can still comment without disappearing in the middle of the night, at least for the time being.

A proposed alternative heath care plan by the

republicans: Stupid, stupid, stupid, here we go again. Just like I think Romney had his election won, all he had to do was lock down on two or three things. Things that republicans never lose on, but no, he just like McCain and Dole tried to out pander the liberals and Dem's.

All he had to do was stay on "Lower taxes, more jobs, and strong national defense," instead of being all over the place pandering and appealing to those that will never vote for a republican in a million years. If he had stayed with the said three things he would have gotten the three million republican votes that stayed at home.

Now, I hear about some supposedly conservative plan to present an alternative health care plan to Obamacare. Dumb, dumb, dumb, how dumb can one get. That would be a toss up to a gleeful socialist press and they would hit it out of the park.

They would focus on it like a laser and drumbeat on how bad it is. All you would hear from them is this is what you can expect from them mean old republicans. What is going to win the 2014 election is future expectations and right now anything is better than more Obamacare.

So, the dumbest thing conservative can do is present a target, good or bad. Never forget, the mass media is socialist and not free and objective anymore. All they need is a real target then one way or another they will make it bad. And that will be the only future expectation as far as the media is concerned. My advice to conservatives, if you have a plan shut the hell up about it until you have the power to install it, in this hostile climate.

"CURSE OF THE "NEW DEAL"
Starting with the "New deal" the liberals seize control of this great country and it's been down hill for them ever since. How they did it, they took the tax payers money and bought vote by handing out goodies, and is still doing it.

It allowed them to gain and keep power, sure, the republicans slip in occasionally but liberals control this great country. Look at our food supply, there are too few people raising and growing food in the USA. That comes from having a minimum wage law.

That is wage control and any wage control won't let wages seek its own level in our free market place economy. Having a minimum wage law guarantees that the USA economy can't be saved no matter what is done. You can enact any law, make any tax change, still, nothing can save the USA economy as long as we have a minimum wage law in place.

The reason is a free market must have some means of balancing itself and a minimum wage law prevents that. The reason the prices of everything you buy is so high is because government subsides prices by giving out tax payer's money on an individual basis.

That-a-work until the whole thing spiral out of control which won't be very long, now. A minimum wage law is like closing off the pop off valve on your hot water heater, then if it over heats, there is no way to bleed off all of the pressure in an emergency.

That means it's gonna blow and almost nothing will be saved. That is the condition of the USA economy, it is fixing to blow us all the way back to the Stone Age. And the sad part is it is all due to ignorance and stupidity.

Repealing the minimum wage law would bleed off the pressure and the USA would survive with only a miserable rebirth taking place, instead of ceasing to exist. Cry me a river, and the beat goes on.
SIRMANS LOG: 27 FEBRUARY 2014, 1537 HOURS

THE VENTING OF A FREEDOM LOVING AMERICAN!!!
Well it's done, there is no doubt left, the

shallow minded liberals has placed the comfort of the welfare state above national security. The choice is no surprise to me. We will soon be like Western Europe, which lacks the military ability to even transport troops to the battle field.

If these liberals keep power, given enough time the USA will be taken over without a bullet being fired. To me it is simple, once the "New deal" programs seized the social and family provider role for itself from the traditional nuclear family head of household the die was cast.

Now, around eighty years later we are fast running out of enough people with the judgment and common sense to remain a free people. We must repeal the minimum wage law to kick the welfare state out of its all powerful family provider role.

It is our last hope; otherwise we will soon be at each others throat to the point that the people will be demanding the iron fist. Like all great nations we are allowing ourselves to be destroyed from within.

The reason you can't survive on the minimum wage is because you have a forced minimum wage in the first place. If you didn't have a forced minimum wage law, out of sight consumer inflation couldn't exist and $5.00 would buy a weeks worth of grocery. Plus, there would be enough jobs for all.

The shallow minded liberals has certainly screwed up this great nation. And if you disagree, guess who held on to the U.S. house of Representative for 40 consecutive years. Also, guess who controls the mass media, education, and almost every institution in America today?

SIRMANS LOG: 24 FEBRUARY 2014, 2105 HOURS

RAISE THE MINIMUM WAGE FOOLS ARE RUSHING IN WHERE WISE MEN REFUSE TO GO.

Anyone that calls for raising the minimum wage doesn't understand a free market place economy, period. The fact is if the USA is to survive, instead of raising the minimum wage it must be repealed entirely. Vamoose, gone, no more government wage or price control, period.

Large or small any business in America has the freedom to raise wages as high as it see fit. But, the minute the government forces any business to raise or lower wages or prices in any manner we no longer has a free market place economy, period. In my view it is sheer ignorance, you either have a free market place economy or you don't.

Throughout history a true free market place

economy has never failed, its boom and bust cycle is a natural process the same as the birth and death cycle. A healthy functioning society is far more than money and how much one makes. In fact, in terms of long term survival trade and bartering is far more important than a currency.

The American Indian and many other societies survived in large numbers and never had a set currency. But, no society has ever survived very long without a strong nuclear and extended family system. Those with money and power hates the boom and bust cycle because they may end up losing everything.

However, nature must have some way of getting rid of inefficiency, moral decay, and culture rot. Sometimes only the bust cycle can purge out too powerful anti-survival forces like the USA has today.

Just look at the condition of the USA, no law or anything is powerful enough to deal with our problems except nature's boom and bust cycle. The world has been rescued from many dynasties only by nature's birth and death cycle.

I keep yelling and hollering that we must get government out of its seized social and family provider role because that has all but destroyed our nuclear and extended family system. And repealing the minimum wage law will allow our nuclear and extended family system to rebound and allow the people to take care of themselves.

A long over due bust cycle is approaching on the horizon and without a strong nuclear family system we can't survive it. I am blessed with this great wisdom and I see it so clearly, that is why I plead so hard that we must get prepared.

We must repeal the minimum wage law, that will restore our strong nuclear and extended family system, our culture, and at least some bartering capacity to survive. Otherwise, we won't have any chance except back to the Stone Age when this teetering economy totally collapses, soon.

SIRMANS LOG: 23 FEBRUARY 2014, 1452 HOURS

WE HAVE A MOB RULED WELFARE STATE OUT OF CONTROL!

Extreme political polling is the worse thing that can happen to a free country. It defeats the reason to have a republic. None of the founding fathers wanted a pure democracy because they all knew in reality it is mob rule with the most flamboyant and smoothest talkers chosen as leaders.

That is the reason they all insisted on a

republic form of government. However, that was long before extreme political polling came along. These were men of great depth and wisdom they knew that the general public is almost never right on anything.

As a rule the general public is uninformed, emotional, and lacks patience, which is a terrible way to govern a nation. So, they all thought by establishing a republic form of government the fear of a mob ruled nation was put to rest forever. Now, lets fast forward to the year of our Lord two thousand fourteenth year, we are almost totally mob ruled all because of extreme political polling.

In a republic the people are suppose to choose leaders that will lead and educate the general public on what is in the best interest of the nation and its long term survival. But today it is just the opposite; we have politicians using extreme political polling to pander to the whims and special interest of the general public.

Even worse, we no longer have a free press standing guard, they are cheer leaders at the socialist parade. A statesman is someone that can only be found in the history books. The thing that the founding fathers feared the most has come to pass, our leadership is chosen from the most flamboyant, smoothest talkers, and those with the best gift of gab and ability to pander to the voters.

Sorry Benjamin Franklin, Sir, we have lost the great Republic you and the founding fathers left for us to keep and safe guard. What we have now is a mob ruled welfare state out of control. To be enlighten read Freddie L Sirmans Sr. books, it is all there. **SIRMANS LOG: 16 FEBRUARY 2014, 2045 HOURS**

THANK GOD! FINALLY! A PLAN TO BOOM THE USA ECONOMY AND CREATE JOBS, JOBS GALORE!
Listen up America; we are on the brink of losing our great USA. So, I felt the need to write this article on what I feel must be done to help save this great nation. Folks, I am a writer and not even a famous or well known one at that. I have no power or influence to speak of.

I am just a lone handicapped neurotic self-made two finger pecking writer. Some even feel I'm off my rocker, too extreme, and should be totally ignored. Maybe so, but the proof of the pudding is in the taste, be your own taster.

Anyone familiar with my writing knows that I have long advocated the repeal of the minimum wage law. And I also think government should abandon its role as a mass social and family provider. I am sure those are the two main things that have brought the USA economy to the brink of total destruction. And by the same token those two things have bred the USA into a government dependent nation.

I know it's futile to expect my ideas to be taken seriously; still I feel I have done my part just by sharing. I believe the mass infusion of government money on an "Individual basis" is what's destroying the USA economy. Doing that destroys the natural balance between the merchant (seller) and the consumer (buyer), thereby causing cost of living inflation.

The reason the middle class is not spending is they don't have the money because of cost of living killing inflation. With that being the case to me the solution is obvious, get the "Individual basis" out of the formula.

There are many ways to do that, in the past I have suggested government set up its own government run commissaries, housing, and clinics. And require the use of tokens or script for all who qualifies. However, I no longer advocate using that system because of start up and other costs.

What I now recommend is government setup a contract type system to separate government "Individual Basis" spending from the national free market place economy. This new recommended system is ready to go and can be put in into place immediately, everything is practically already in place. The use of food stamps is well established.

Remember the key to eliminating the "Individual basis" from the national free market place economy is separation. So, all government has to do is contract with retailers for set aside stores for food stamp use only.

That will stop the upward cost of living spiral in its tracts, then the buying power of ones paycheck will buy much, much more and the middle class will be able to save again.

Also, these government stores must accept only EBT or some other type of government card or it will defeat the purpose. Once the government stores are up and operating then EBT and other government cards can only be used in those stores.

This separate retail system could be tested in one state, e.g. Michigan. And if successful, then extend to housing and clinics, and if still successful then go nation wide. Without a doubt this system will boom the USA economy and put people back to work on a large scale, plus save our dying economy.

However, don't hold your breath, politics is in everything, and what I believe will save the economy and this great country may never see the light of day.

However, the cold hard fact is either the USA takes this plan serious and change course, or I will guarantee you the USA will soon be sold off piece meal to foreigners. Being $17,000,000,000,000,000,000 in debt makes the USA a beggar, and you know the old saying: Beggars can't be choosey. There is no doubt about it the country will soon be sold off.

SIRMANS LOG: 25 JANUARY 2014, 1702 HOURS

USA SURVIVAL ANALYSIS JANUARY 2014
Here is my Freddie L Sirmans, Sr. analysis on the state of the USA survival. I will say up front the USA can be saved as a free nation with private property rights and individual freedom still intact. But, I don't believe the USA has a snowball chance in hell of surviving another five years as a free sovereign nation with the course we are currently on.

I believe because of our debt ($17,000,000,000,000,000,000) and reckless spending the USA will be sold off piece meal to foreign nations. Our government at all cost will try to hold on to its social and family provider role. If not that we will lose our individual freedom and private property right and come under some type of authoritarian rule.

This liberal induced welfare state has run it course, it's over, something gotta give. Reality have set in and will not be denied. Let me say again the USA can be saved. We have two major political parties, However, I am an independent with conservative leaning. The USA is the only home I know and my whole focus is the survival of my beloved country.

I have voted Democrat many times, I even voted for Jimmy Carter and George McGovern. In my analysis I will stay with the terms liberals or conservatives. So brace yourself and hang on. I feel the liberal mindset has all but destroyed this great land of the free and home of the braved that the founding fathers laid out.

Of course the liberals will totally disagree with me on this, they believe they have greatly helped the poor and made life easier for everyone. And, I will not for one second disagree, who could disagree with that, because it is true. But, that is the trap and where my great depth and wisdom comes into play.

I have said it before and will say it again. The only way government can help the very poor and needy without destroying our culture, our economy, and eventually our country is to establishing government run commissaries, houses, and clinics with the use of coupons or scripts for all who qualify.

Government spending on an individual basis must always be kept separated from the national economy or inflation will eventually spiral out of control. It is on the individual basis that government money destroys the natural balance between the merchant (seller) and the customer (buyer).

That is what ignites and causes inflation in a free market place. And is the reason the cost of living (prices) far out distances the earnings from the workers labor.

Government can spend all it wants and it won't drive up the cost of living as long as it is not handed out on an individual basis. That is why the use of coupons or script is a must to keep government individual spending separated from the real economy. And things like food stamps or whatever is used must never be spent with the free market place merchants. because that is what is driving the cost of everything for the working man/woman out of reach now.

Back to the truth about liberals helping the poor. Sure they help the poor, but, my God, at what a price. Their method is leaving almost no survival tools in place after four generations. We have almost no strong nuclear and extended family system left. We have almost no sense of morality left.

Plus, we have almost no small farmers and home gardeners left to provide emergency bartering capacity if money become worthless, which is highly likely. Morality today means same sex marriages and killing in the womb on demand, if that don't mean suicide to long term survival I'll be a monkeys uncle.

It is like selling your sole for riches and pleasure. Destroying the system itself should always be avoided, but that is exactly what the liberal's mindset has done. They took the course of least resistance and have destroyed a system that has served mankind for over 6000 year.

All of our eggs are in one basket, this phony economy could collapse any day now and there are no survival tools to keep the USA from regressing all the way back to the Stone Age. The two deadly and unforgivable sins the liberals committed are number one they seized the social and family provider role for the government itself.

That act took away the survival need for the strong nuclear and extended family system. According to nature's supreme law of natural selection everything that exists must have a survival need or it starts ceasing to exist. The second deadly sin was to enact and put in place a minimum wage law.

That act gave the government total power and control over private property rights, all production, and the distribution of products. In fact the welfare state couldn't exist without the minimum wage law. It would have no way of corrupting the free market place by inflating the money supply enough to continue reckless spending.

Ninety nine percent of the general public sees the minimum wage law only in terms of the size of their pay check, but that is a facade that disguises the absolute power it gives the government over free enterprise. So, as for who can save this great country, in terms of liberals saving it, ridicules, first the country must be saved from the liberals.

Now, as to the role of the conservatives, bless their hearts they means well. But, they don't even come close to being willing by hook or crook to match liberals for getting power. Plus, conservative think they can cut spending and still save our welfare state, trust me that ain't gonna happen.

It's far too much water over the bridge in my view for this welfare state to ever be saved. Besides, politically speaking all spending cuts is going to do is guarantee liberals stay in power. My suggestion for conservatives is go with the flow until you get in power and then repeal the minimum wage law.

But, do like the liberals never tell your true intentions just get in there and repeal it. The problem with my suggestion is: The conservatives totally disagrees with me, they have been seduced and think they need to save this welfare state and if anything raise the minimum wage, not repeal it. Government must be returned to its role before the "New deal," repealing the minimum wage law will do that.

So, like I have said before only a miracle can save the USA from total doom. However, I do believe in miracles.

SORRY BENJAMIN FRANKLIN SIR, LIBERAL POLICY HAS DESTROYED YOUR BELOVED REPUBLIC!

There is an old saying, those that lives on hope dies fasting. The great republic that Benjamin Franklin and others founding fathers left us no longer exist due to insane liberal policy. The most stupid and insane of all is not having an official national language.

That is kindergarten wisdom type of thinking, it is sheer ignorance, down the road there is no way in hell we can keep this great nation as one being bi-language. With all of our different races, religions, and other factors, only one unifying language can keep the USA intact.

Yet, where there is no real national violent or disunity problem we freely toss lasting unity out the window by installing another language, all because new deal liberal policy has corrupted our culture.

Before the "New deal" the people would have been up in arms over something so dumb and stupid, down the road even an idiot knows only one national language will keep the USA from splitting apart. When the British made English the official national language of India even the Indians themselves said it was a good thing.

Yet, here we are in the USA voluntary doing something dumb and stupid like this that is guaranteed to cause mass violence and disruption down the road, unbelievable. It's over folks; we have already lost this great country due to liberal policy.

Today, we are not only reaping the economically seed sown by the liberal new deal programs, we are also reaping the almost total destruction of our culture. And the saddest of all is how so many young minds of the very young are being twisted with anti-survival hogwash on TV.

Is Immigration A Blessing In Disguise?

It is so much harder for young minds to know the different from what is real and normal than it is for adults; the very young see hogwash as the way life is and should be. In my opinion we have lost this great nation, the great USA.

Can we take it back; sure, it's simple, just repeal the minimum wage law and stop government from giving out money on an individual basis. I have been saying that for years, but political no one wants to hear that.

Believe it or not, but it is just that simple; otherwise soon the country will be sold off to foreigners because of $17,000,000,000,000,000,000 in debt. how sad.

I have been called extreme and the odd man out. But, the gospel truth of the matter is I am really the wise and sane one in terms of raw long term survival. The moral decay and culture rot that the USA has today has been the last stage throughout history before a civilization experiences total doom.

I believe if you spare the rod you spoil the child. Some people think that is being mean and uncaring to a child. I think it is just the opposite because when done properly paddling instills the strongest conscience in a child. But, the truth of the matter is there is no single best way to raise a child.

I believe physical disciplined instills a stronger conscience and a better sense of self-restraint in a child. I believe a lack of self-restraint is why African American men commit crimes far out of proportion for their number. "A stitch in time will save nine," or a lick on the behind in time will keep a kid out of prison way past age nine plus nine.

After the "New deal" the welfare state kicked the poor Black man out of the home. I think that act have caused most black youths to grow up with very little self-restraint, and with each succeeding generation the problem has grown worse.

Sure, some single Black moms can take care of business on that behind, but most can't or won't.

SIRMANS LOG: 05 FEBRUARY 2014, 1319 HOURS

WRITERS BELIEF ON KNOWLEDGE AND THE WORKING OF THE HUMAN KIND.
I don't care how many books one reads or how much education one has; genuine deep wisdom comes only through physical or emotional hardship and struggle. Still, hardship and struggle won't make everyone a Sage or saint, some people just naturally goes against the grain and will become even bitterer.

It is just not possible for most people to understand my thinking; they haven't paid the price that is why I can only thank God for the way he made me. It may not show but super achievers are almost always searching for love, approval, or to be accepted in some way.

Those feeling loved and contented tend to stay on course as just ordinary achievers. Please don't get it twisted; I still think ones first priority in life is to get the best education possibly.

USA FIRST LINE OF DEFENSE NEWS MEDIA HAS LOST ITS WAY, HOW SAD.

I remember as a young teenager back in the late 1950's learning about propaganda and how the communist kept their citizens ignorant from true facts. I felt how blessed we were in America to have a free press that could always be trusted with: just the facts ma'am, just the facts.

Well, I can only speak for myself and think for myself, But, in my view the liberals and Dem's are far better propagandist than the communist ever were. They just flat out refuse to stand up and face any blame for this nation destroying insane Obamacare disaster that have been forced upon this great nation, we may not even financially survive it.

Yet, they are fixing to try and place blame for it anywhere other than themselves, we are a forgiving people, man up for once. Thank God we have a counterforce against the liberals and Dem's thrust. Otherwise, this administration with its bratty liberal news media cohorts riding shotgun would have taken the country into full socialism by now.

I think the predominately liberal news media is like a bunch of teenage brats that think they have all of the answers to everything. But, in truth can't see past their noses. This country is $17, 000,000,000,000,000,000 in debt and will soon be sold off piece meal to foreigners. And where do you think our first line of defense is at?

They are at the socialist parade whooping and hollering it up as cheer leaders while the financial health of the country goes to hell in a hand basket. My advice which I don't expect to be taken is to anyone that the liberals and Dem's sic their liberal news media attack dogs on, stand your ground proud because you are doing the job they are suppose to be doing.

That is standing guard and protecting this great land of individual freedom from socialism or any other ism.
SIRMANS LOG: 24 JANUARY 2014, 1349

HOURS

BOOK 2, A GREAT LITTLE FABLE I WROTE SEVERAL YEARS AGO.

Chapter 1

Once upon a time there was a little town called Health-land kingdom, located right off the big super MD highway leading to the great cure-all metropolis. In this town lived vitamins, minerals,   herbs, humans, and other nutrients.

The town's main goal was to keep all of its citizens healthy because anyone that   they failed to keep healthy would have to face terrible traffic jams on the super MD highway leading to the great cure-all metropolis.

Jim-Niacin (vitamin B-3). Jim-Niacin doesn't stand alone; he is a member of the very powerful B vitamin family. In Health-land Jim-Niacin's job is essential to promote life and good health. He regulates the metabolism and assists in other body processes, even though he is needed in small amounts compared to proteins and carbohydrates.

Is Immigration A Blessing In Disguise?

As a coenzyme Jim-Niacin works
to make sure the human body
functions as it should. There are two
major types of vitamins: the water
soluble and the oil soluble. Jim-Niacin
belongs to the water-soluble type vitamins,
therefore his doses
must be replaced everyday because
the human body doesn't store his
doses like the oil soluble type.

Since Jim-Niacin is only one
member of the very powerful B
vitamin family he shouldn't work
alone; he should be balanced with
other B vitamin members. Jim-Niacin
is not a bad or evil fellow, but he does
have a bad reputation.

Humans are afraid of Jim-Niacin
and rightly so because in too high
doses he may damage the liver, or in
too low doses he does no good. But,
that is not the only reason human
fear Jim-Niacin. Jim-Niacin deals with
circulation and the skin, and he will
heat the skin up like it is on fire and
turn it as red as a beet.
When this happens to a human
for the first time, it will scare some
humans half to death, but don't be put
off, the flushing of the skin is normal
when dealing with Jim-Niacin. It's not
pretty or pleasant but that is how Jim-

Niacin unclogs the capillaries and
small blood vessels throughout the
body.

Captain Fredrico (human). Orry
Fredrico is one of many humans that
Was born and raised in Health-land
Kingdom. Orry Fredrico is a
Carpenter by trade, but as long as he
Could remember he loved the sea.
As a small child he would stand by
The ocean for hours just staring out to
Sea.
As a teenager he would try to
Hop aboard any boat going salt water
Fishing. During his senior year in high
School he went on one of those deep
Sea fishing cruises that goes out for
Four or five hours at a time. On this
Cruises he met Jan Flemmings. Jan
Also loved the sea and they instantly
Became attracted to each other.
Within days Jim started dating Jan.

VC (vitamin C). VC also belongs
To the water-soluble type of vitamin.
VC   is truly a heavyweight among
Vitamins. VC is known as a very
Power antioxidant. He is a mighty
Human body protector. He protects
the human body against harmful
effects of pollution. He helps to
prevent cancer. He helps to lower

cholesterol and other protection functions.

Scurvy is a disease that moves in when there is a deficiency in vitamin C protection. Years ago, passengers on ships on long voyages without fresh fruits and vegetables had a problem dealing with scurvy.

Jan Flemmings (human). Jan is a Health-land Kingdom toy soldier's brat. Just like Captain Fredrico she has always loved the sea. She was mostly unanchored until she met her soul mate Orry Fredrico. At first she thought he loved the sea too much and would not be a good provider, but his dreamy bedroom eyes soon won her over.

VE (vitamin E). VE belongs to the oil soluble type of vitamin. VE is another mighty antioxidant. VE is very important in fighting cancer and cardiovascular disease. Vitamin E is a giant in so many ways. VE is a natural blood thinner. He promotes good blood circulation, he promotes healthy skin, healthy hair, and so many other healthy body functions. Vitamin E actually belongs to a family of eight but falls into two major groups. These two groups are tocopherols and tocotrienols. It is the alpha-tocopherols form that is the most potent. That is the group VE belongs to.

John-Pyridoxine (vitamin B-6). John-Pyridoxine like his cousin Jim-Niacin is a member of the very powerful B vitamin family. The fact is John-Pyridoxine is involved in more bodily functions than any other single nutrient. John-Pyridoxine deals with both the mental and physical health.

He deals with water retention, sodium and potassium balance, and fights hard against allergies, arthritis, asthma, carpal tunnel syndrome, and on and on. Just like his cousin Jim-Niacin, John-Pyridoxine shouldn't fight alone; he should be balanced with other members of the mighty B vitamin family.

Mister Disease. Mister and his family   showed up one day in Health-land Kingdom. No one seems to know where he came from. All anyone knows is he is mean and evil. He has no friends and is known to

attack humans sometimes without
provocation.

He has no conscience and will
attack anyone that is weak and
helpless. The town and kingdom has
tried to keep him out, but somehow
he always sneaks back in. Our
vitamins, minerals, herbs and others
nutrient citizens have done a good job
fighting him off, but Mister Disease is
a very, very tough customer.

      Jim-Niacin and the other nutrient
protectors of Health-land Kingdom
were joyfully patting themselves on
the back because they were doing a
good job protecting the city's
population from Mister Disease and
his cohorts. Jim-Niacin decided to
telephone his cousin John-Pyridoxine.
Jim could hear the phone making its
fourth ring.

"Hello," said John-Pyridoxine.
" This is Jim-Niacin, I decided to
give you a call and touch base on a
matter that I've been tossing around
in my mind lately."
"Tell me about it," said John-
Pyridoxine.

"Well, I've been thinking that all

of the vitamins, minerals, humans, herbs, and other nutrient citizens should get together and have a big town hall meeting. What do you think."

"I think it is a very good idea," said john-Pyridoxine.
" Good, then it's a go, I'm going to start right away making plans," said Jim-Niacin. "John you take care now, I'll talk to you later."
" Bye," said John-Pyridoxine.

Chapter 2

Orry Fredrico and Jan Flemmings got married after a one year engagement. Orry got an associate degree in carpentry from the local technical college. Twenty five years later Orry and Jan are now the parents of a seventeen-year-old son Rob, and a fifteen-year-old daughter Melinda.

Almost everyone calls Orry   by his nickname Captain Fredrico after he bought his first boat about fifteen years ago. The boat was a fourteen footer with a big Mercury motor. Captain Fredrico now operates his own contracting business.

Is Immigration A Blessing In Disguise?

It is almost six o'clock p.m. when
Captain Fredrico lets himself in the
carport door which opens directly into
the kitchen. He found his wife Jan
bending over checking her meat loaf
in the oven.

"Hello dear," said Captain
Fredrico in a somewhat tired voice.
" Hello Orry, how did your day
" Pretty good, but my right wrist
that's been bothering me the last
couple of weeks seems to be getting
worse, especially at night after I fall
asleep.   Sometimes I wake up with a
numb tingling in my right hand. It
feels like somebody is sticking pins in
my hands."

"Orry, I think you need to check
with one of the vitamin citizens. That
sounds like something John-
pyridoxine might be able to help you
with."

"I think you are right dear, I will
give him a call in a few days.

       After Marrying Orry, Jan Fredrico
decided to postpone a career of her
own. Becoming a full time housewife
and mother was very fulfilling to Jan.

She even took on the   awesome job
of home schooling her kids.

VC (vitamin c) enjoys his job in
Health-land Kingdom taking care of
its citizens. He has a very good
reputation. Humans were using him
probably more than any other vitamin.
Being one of the most powerful
antioxidants, he was in great demand
these days.

In fact, he was being used to
fortify many of today's foods. He
thought the town hall meeting was a
great idea. Why didn't he think of it?
The vitamins and other nutrients were
doing a good job fighting off Mister
Disease, but he knew that they
couldn't let their guards down, ever.

Just like VC, VE (vitamin E) is
another very powerful antioxidant but
of the oil soluble type. VE is probably
in even greater demand these days
than VC. With so many humans
becoming diabetics these days, VE
with his natural blood thinning power
is a real workhorse. VE is also
looking forward to the big town hall
meeting coming up soon.

Is Immigration A Blessing In Disguise?

On this Monday morning John-Pyridoxine was kicking back at his office when the phone ring.
" Hello," said John-Pyridoxine.
" May I speak to John-Pyridoxine?" said the voice on the line.

"This is he," said John-Pyridoxine.
" I'm Captain Fredrico and I've been told you may be able to help me concerning an ailment. I believe I have a case of carpal tunnel syndrome."

"You have the right vitamin, that is one of my many areas of expertise."
" Then you will be able to help me," said Captain Fredrico.

"Hold on a minute, I didn't say that. Let me explain the situation here, then I can tell you what I may be able to do. Listen Captain, I'm going to explain what I do, and it should take care of your problem, but then it may not. If I can't cure it, then I recommend you take the super MD highway to the cure all metropolis."

"I understand," said Captain

Fredrico.
" Now, first off," said John-
Pyridoxine, "my maximum dose is
300 mg. per day, that way I will not
damage any nerves. In most cases
100 mg. of my dose will cure the
problem. The golden rule with taking
any nutrients is don't take more than
the recommended dose, because too
much of anything may cause
damage, and never take nutrients on
an empty stomach. So, Captain if
you understood everything I said,
come by as soon as possible. We
have a walk in policy."

"Thank you sir, I should be there
within the hour."

Mister Disease is very upset with
himself for being unable to do more
damage in Health-land Kingdom. He
feels he should be able to bring in
more of his friends like cancer, AIDS,
and even some of his very old friends
like the black plague.

He was getting fed up with those
damn vitamins, minerals, herbs, and
other nutrients. The thing about
those nutrients is they are keeping
him from getting a foothold in Health-
land Kingdom. He feels that if he

could just get a foothold he would be able to start an epidemic.

Mister Disease decided that he would just have to work harder. Sooner or later those humans are going to think that they are safe and slack up on utilizing the nutrients. That is the time he plans to throw his best punch. He feels that if his friend AIDS just keeps up the pressure, he has the best shot at causing an epidemic.

Most humans don't know Jim-Niacin and many of those that do tend to fear and avoid him. As one of the smallest members of the powerful B vitamin family, being unknown is about to change. The reason is Jim-Niacin along with his cousin John-Pyridoxine are the ones that called for and organized the town hall meeting coming up in a few weeks. The whole thing was originally Jim-Niacin's idea.

Since then Jim has invited the town fathers and secured all of the permits needed to stage such an event. Jim has contacted other town nutrients and humans,

many of them had never heard of
him, or knew who he was.

Chapter 3

Captain Fredrico had lived in
Health-land Kingdom all of his life and
he loved this town. Captain Fredrico
got an invitation from Jim-Niacin to
attend the town hall meeting coming
up in a few weeks.

Captain Fredrico had heard the
name Jim-Niacin before and even
knew he was a member of the mighty
B vitamin family, but that was about
all he knew about Jim-Niacin. He
didn't know what kind of work or
anything else Jim-Niacin did.

Captain Fredrico had heard that
the vitamins and other nutrients
citizens had become concerned about
the health of Health-land Kingdom.
The main work our nutrient citizens
do is protect our human population
from characters like Mister Disease
and his friends.

The nutrients knew that cancer
and AIDS had almost destroyed a few
other towns in the Kingdom. The
town hall meeting got Captain

Is Immigration A Blessing In Disguise?

Fredrico to thinking. The mayoral
election will be coming up in about a
year. Captain Fredrico decided that
he was going to throw his hat in the
ring. Of course he would have to talk
it over with his wife Jan first.

After putting in a hard day's
work, on his drive home Captain
Fredrico thought about the pesky dry
skin that had been plaguing him for
years. It has slowly become more
and more of a problem as time past.

Now it has become a real nuisance.
It has come to the point that he has
to lotion down almost his whole body
every time he takes a shower.
He feels that is unmanly, only
women like to lotion their bodies. He
has tried everything, but to no avail.

He had even got on the crowded
super MD highway and went to the
cure all metropolis, but still to no
avail. At the cure all metropolis all
they did was to prescribe an
extremely expensive body cream that
did little better than over the counter
creams.

He felt truly at his wits end.
There didn't seem to be any hope, he
would just have to accept his

miserable fate. As Captain Fredrico
let himself in the carport door, Jan
was making a salad.
" Hello, dear," said the Captain in
a husky sexy voice.

"Hello, sweetheart," said Jan in
a wooing voice as she dropped
everything and rushed over and
planted a seductive kiss on her
husband's left cheek.

"Now, you go ahead and clean
up, dinner will be ready in a few
minutes. By the way Rob complained
about a bout of indigestion after
lunch."

"Did you check with Mr. Blue
Page?" said the Captain.
" Yes, he gave me the names of
several nutrients that work in that
area. The two nutrients that I decided
to use were Stewart-Ginger Root and
Henry-Acidolphilus. Each one of
them gave me heavy doses to give
Rob as needed."

"Good, now let me go ahead
and wash up, then you can tell me all
about it later." After the Captain and
all of the family had sat down to
dinner and the blessing was said, the
Captain revisited the subject of Rob's

indigestion.

"How is your stomach feeling
now, Rob," said the Captain.
" It's fine now, dad, since Mom
had a couple of the nutrients treat it."
" I wasn't sure what to do until
after my talk with Mr. Blue Page,"
said Jan.

"Mr. Blue Page gave me the
names of several nutrients that work
in the area of indigestion. These are
the names that Mr. Blue Page gave
me that deal with indigestion:
Stewart-Ginger Root, Calvin-
Fenugreek, Bonnie-Papaya, Henry-
Acidophilus, and Sammy-Oat bran
tablets.

He also stressed that they did
their work with either tablets or
capsules."

"Excuse me for changing the
subject, I have a very important
announcement to make," said the
captain.

"Jan, the mayoral election is
coming up in about a year and I
would like to know if you have any
objections to me throwing my hat into
the ring."

"Gee, I don't know? I've never
thought about being a politician's wife.
Do you think you can win?"
"Dad, I love it, I think it is a great
idea," said Melinda.
"Me too," said Rob.

"I can't guarantee you I will win,
but I believe if I get out there and
shake enough hands I'll have a very
good shot."
" Dad, I'll campaign for you," said
Melinda.

"Honey, If you really want to
run, then count me in as your number
one supporter," said Jan.
"Then it's all settled You are
looking at the next mayor of Health-
land Kingdom."

Ever since John-Pyridoxine had
agreed to help his cousin Jim-Niacin
organize the big town hall meeting
coming up soon, he had stayed busy
calling and talking to the citizens of
Health-land Kingdom.

Chapter 4

Mr. Disease was aware of the
big town hall meeting coming up in a

few days, and he definitely was not
pleased about what he was hearing.
The word was they were going to try
to get rid of him. Mr. Disease was
not going to let that deter him, that
had been tried before with his
ancestors all throughout history.

Sure, the discovery of DDT,
penicillin, and modern antibiotics had
given his family some big setbacks,
but some of his old friends like
tuberculosis were beginning to make
a comeback, and the new kid on the
block, AIDS, was really beginning to
raise hell.

Mr. Disease felt that as far as he
was concerned, let them have all of
the town hall meetings they want to, it
was not going to put him out of
business.

Mr. Disease watches the
super MD highway often and as far
as he could tell it was becoming even
more crowded each day. Even at the
big super cure all metropolis they
haven't been able to get rid of his
best friend Mr. Cancer. Mr. Cancer is
still doing an awful lot of damage.

On this Monday morning Jan

Is Immigration A Blessing In Disguise?

Fredrico   sure didn't want to battle the traffic jams on the super MD highway going to the cure all metropolis. It was just one of those days, Her daughter was down with a cold and she herself was dealing with a slight kidney infection.

She didn't know? Maybe it was something she ate that was causing her back a slight ache in the area of her kidney. She knew that it would save her a lot of money and time if she called Mr. Blue Page and found out which vitamins, minerals, herbs, or other nutrients that specialized in the areas of their ailments.

Jan decided to give the nutrients twenty-four hours to do their work, then if there was no obvious improvement she would get on the crowded super MD highway to the cure all metropolis. Jan dialed Mr. Blue Page. The voice on the line said, " You have reached Mr. Blue Page directory."
"Mr. Blue Page, this is Jan Fredrico.   My daughter has a cold and my kidneys have a slight ache. I would like for you to give me the names of the nutrients that specialize in the areas of our illness."

"Very well, madam. In the area
of the   kidneys, the association of
VC and Cranberry handle that, and
in the area of colds and flu, the
association of Garlic, Echinacea, and
Golden Seal handle that.   Will that be
all, madam?"

"Yes sir, and thank you very
much," said Jan. Taking advantage
of their-walk in policy, Jan didn't have
to wait long before she was able to
see VC, the very powerful vitamin C
antioxidant.

"Mrs. Fredrico," said VC, " We
give our doses in mostly tablet form.
I am of the water soluble type, the
body does not store my doses.
Taking too much of my dose is
washed out with the urine. But,
taking too much of my dose also may
cause diarrhea or stomach soreness
in some humans.

Rule number one for dealing with
your kidney problem is to keep
drinking lots of water, then take 2000
mg. of vitamin C tablets three or four
times a day after a meal, also take
2000 mg. of cranberry fruit capsules
three of four times a day after a meal.
That should take care of your
problem, Mrs. Fredrico."

Jan next proceeded to take her
daughter by the association of Garlic,
Echinacea, and Golden Seal to take
care of her cold. After a short wait
Jan and her daughter were lead in to
see Hannah-Garlic.

Hannah-Garlic came from one of
the most powerful and popular of all
herb families. Even   the Roman
army would not go into battle without
a member of the garlic family coming
along.

Hannah-Garlic instructed Jan to
give Melinda throat lozenges if
needed, then give her a dose of about
1400 mg. of odor controlled garlic,
three or four times a day after a meal,
also give her a 1500 mg. dose of
combination echinacea-golden seal
three or four times a day after a meal.

"You should see some obvious
improvement in twenty four hours; if
not take the super MD highway to the
cure all metropolis.

"It is also helpful to take heavy
doses of vitamin C after a meal at the
beginning of a cold. But, only at the
beginning of a cold, because if
congestion sets in, vitamin C tends

to make it worse. Warning: Never
take vitamin C or others nutrients on
an empty stomach," she said.
After thoroughly going over
everything, Hannah-Garlic said, "
That is it, Mrs. Fredrico, do you
understand all of my instructions?"

"Yes, Herb Garlic and thank you
very much." While driving home Jan
reminded herself to do her neck
exercises when she got home. It has
been quite awhile since stress has
caused her neck to tense up, but she
Decided that she would go ahead
and do the exercises anyway.

Jan believed that feeling stress is
a normal part of life. The better one
learns how to deal with life's
frustrations the better one will be able
to cope with stress. Stress affects
people in many different ways. It
may affect some in physical ways
such as headaches, neck aches,
shoulder aches, etc.

To deal with physical aches it is
helpful to do these exercises. These
exercises are done sitting on the side
of the bed. Sit on the side of the bed
with feet apart flat on the floor for
balance. With both hands rolled into
a fist, place them thumbs inward

down on the bed several inches from the body on each side.

Start the first exercise by twisting the neck and entire upper body counter-clockwise as far as possible, then twist the neck and entire upper body clockwise as far as possible. Do these exercises in sets of one hundred as many times as one desires.

Start the second exercise by leaning the head as far as possible on the right shoulder, then lean the head as far as possible on the left shoulder. Do these exercises in sets of one hundred as many times as one desires.

Start the third exercise by leaning the chin as far as possible down on the chest, then lift the head backward as far as possible. Do these exercises in sets of one hundred as many times as one desires.

Chapter 5

On the morning of the big town hall meeting, Jim-Niacin followed his daily routine of taking care of the

citizens of Health-land Kingdom. Jim-
Niacin tried to take care of all loose
ends concerning the town hall
meeting by making a lot of last minute
phone calls. He rehearsed the
program with his cousin B-12 who
would be the moderator for tonight's
town hall meeting.

At seven o'clock p.m. sharp Jim-
Niacin arrived at the local high school
gymnasium, the location of tonight's
town hall meeting. The meeting was
scheduled to start at eight o'clock
p.m. There were several satellite
trucks already in place when he
arrived. There were the local radio
and TV crews as well as reporters
from the big super cure all metropolis.

Arriving at the high school was
familiar territory for Captain Fredrico.
He had walked at the high school
track three or more times a week for
several years. The high school track
was a popular walking place for the
citizens of Health-land Kingdom.
Captain Fredrico felt that walking or
some type of physical fitness program
is a must to maintain good health.

It is a fact that one in good
physical condition has almost a ten
times better chance of surviving a

heart attack, stroke, or any ailment.
Also, physical activity plays a big role
in controlling diabetes. A big help
with diabetes is controlling what one
eats. Most humans can control
diabetes by cutting way back on
starches and sweets and taking a
chromium picolinate at each meal.

One needs to eat less meat and
include more peas, beans, fresh
fruits, and raw vegetables. One
needs to include at least one raw fruit
or vegetable at each meal because
cooking and microwaving food
destroys all enzymes and most
vitamins.

Enzymes are involved in almost
every bodily function, especially the
digestive process. Enzymes are
mostly divided into two groups:
digestive enzymes and metabolic
enzymes. The digestive enzymes
break down food enabling the body to
function properly.

The human body manufactures a
limited supply of enzymes, but in
order to prevent indigestion and other
digestive problems one should get as
many enzymes as possible from raw
food. Otherwise, the body's limited
supply becomes depleted.

Is Immigration A Blessing In Disguise?

Jim could see that there was
going to be a very big turnout for
tonight's event. It seemed like his
hard work on getting the word out had
paid off. Several tables were set up
at one end of the gymnasium to try
to accommodate as many as possible
on the big panel of vitamins, minerals,
humans, herbs, and other nutrients.

Everyone were handed a
program as they filed into the
gymnasium. It read that, "We will not
be able to accommodate everyone
due to the time it would take. The
moderator will ask all questions, but
he will take a few written questions
from the audience." At exactly eight
p.m. sharp B-12 (vitamin B-12)
strode up to the podium.

"Greetings, my fellow vitamins,
minerals, humans, herbs, and other
nutrients, I'm B-12 your moderator for
tonight's town hall meeting," he said.
"First I would like to welcome our
town's fathers, celebrities, and all
other dignitaries to this town hall
meeting. Now, I would like to thank
the vitamin that made it all happen.
He is truly another unsung hero.
Many of you here tonight probably
have never heard of him, but all of

the while he has been out there
everyday doing his job. He is one of
the lesser known members of the
powerful B vitamin family. I am proud
to say this truly unsung hero is my
first cousin Jim-Niacin (vitamin B-3).
Stand up, Jim."

"Thank you, thank you, thank
you," said Jim-Niacin as he stood and
the audience loudly applauded.
"Now," said B-12, "before we get
into questions and answers we are
going to let several members on our
panel down here give their name and
vocation. We will start with me. I'm
B-12 (vitamin B-12). One of my
many jobs is to assure proper
digestion and the absorption of food."

"I'm Jane-Ginkgo Biloba. I'm a
very well known herb. I'm mostly
Known for improving memory."
"I'm Sammy-Oat Bran Tablets.
I'm known for my fiber. Fiber does so
many things, for now I will mention
just two, I lower the blood cholesterol
and help stabilize blood sugar."

"I'm Eddie-calcium. I'm a mineral
and I do many things. I'm most
needed for strong bones and teeth
and to help lower blood pressure."
"I'm Mary-Magnesium. I'm a

mineral and of the many things that I
do, enzyme activity is most vital. I
also assist calcium and potassium
uptake."

"I'm Sue-Chromium. I'm a
mineral and of the many things that I
do, maintaining stable blood sugar
levels is most vital."
"I'm VA (vitamin A). I'm a
vitamin and lesser known antioxidant.
My main job is protecting the eyes
and some skin problems."
"I'm Dee Dee (vitamin D). I'm a
vitamin, and I'm needed for the
absorption   of calcium and
phosphorus."

"I'm Ned-Zinc. I'm a mineral and
of the many things that I do, keeping
the prostate gland healthy is most
vital."

"I'm Kenny-Saw Pametto. I'm an
herb, my main job is to prevent the
enlargement of the prostate gland."
"I'm Gina-Evening Primrose Oil.
I'm an essential fatty acid. I'm a
necessity that cannot be made by
the human body. I do many things,
but improving the skin is my favorite."

"I'm Patty-Potassium. I'm a
mineral. Of my many jobs I will

name just a few. I help maintain a healthy nervous system and regulate heart rhythm, also I help control the body's water balance."

"I'm Hannah-Garlic. I'm an herb. I detoxify and protect the body against infections. I help lower blood pressure, aid circulation and perform many other functions."

"I'm Henry-Acidophilus. I'm a friendly bacteria. My main job is to aid digestion."

"I'm Bonnie-Papaya. I'm an herb. I aid digestion. I'm good for heartburn, indigestion, and bowel disorders."

"I'm Brad-Cranberry Fruit. I'm an herb. I'm helpful for fighting infections of the urinary track."

"I'm Stewart-Ginger Root. I'm an herb. I do many things, but cleaning the colon, reducing spasms, and stomach cramps is my favorite."

"I'm Calvin-Fenugreek. I'm good for the stomach, intestines, eyes, asthma, sinus, inflammation, and lung disorders. I also increase sexual desire."

"I'm Edna-Echinacea. I'm an
herb. I have anti viral properties
and I help boost the immune system.
I'm very helpful against colds and flu."
"I'm Gene-Golden Seal. I'm an
herb. I act as an antibiotic, and have
anti-inflammatory and antibacterial
properties."

I'm David-Dandelion root. I am
an herb. I help cleanse the blood
stream and liver and increase the
production of bile. I'm used as a
diuretic. I help reduce uric acid and
improve functioning of the stomach
and other vital organs.

"That is the last introduction we
will have time for," said B-12. "Now, I
will ask the panel a few written
questions given to me from the
audience, but first let me explain our
role here. Number one is we try to
be the first line of defense on
protecting Health-land Kingdom from
Mr. Disease and his cohorts.

"We have some citizens who
don't believe in us and won't use our
services. The next thing is we don't
try to be everything to everybody, our
services and abilities are limited.

Is Immigration A Blessing In Disguise?

We encourage anyone that has doubts or don't believe in us to take the super MD highway to the cure all metropolis. Still, there is a lot we can do to keep Mr. Disease and his friends from gaining a foothold here in Health-land Kingdom.

"Very important: When taking the super MD highway to the cure all metropolis, make sure you tell them which of our services you are maintaining.

"Now, when I ask a question to the panel, please let those that specialize in that particular area of expertise answer the question. Time will not allow me to ask but only a few questions. My first question to the panel is what can we do to combat prostate disease?" he asked.
"I'm Ned-Zinc, and I recommend 50 mg. of zinc per day."

"I'm Larry-Pumpkin Seed Oil, and I recommend 1000 mg. of pumpkin seed oil per day."
"I'm Kenny-Saw Pametto, and I recommend 160 mg. of saw pametto extract twice per day."
"I'm VE (vitamin E), and I recommend 1000 I.U. of vitamin E per day."

"I'm Jim-Niacin, and I
recommend my maintenance dose of
250 mg. of niacin per day."
"Is there anyone else?" said B-
12. "So, that gives us five weapons
to fight prostate disease, and I'm
pretty darn sure that anyone that
arms themselves with these weapons
will be able to keep Mr. prostate
disease away for a very long time, if
not forever. My next question to the
panel is what can we do to deal with
diabetes disease?"

"I'm Sue-Chromium, and I
recommend 200 mg. of chromium
picolinate three times a day at meal
time. I also would like to elaborate a
little on this terrible disease.

"Diet plays a   major role in
controlling this terrible disease.
Everyone with this disease should be
able to home check his blood sugar
level and keep it under control. But,
controlling blood sugar is not the only
problem diabetics face.

"There are problems with the
eyes, blood circulation, and many
others. There is a problem with nerve
damage (neuropathy) especially in
the lower extremities," she concluded.

"I'm VE (vitamin E), and I
recommend 1000 I.U. of vitamin E
per day. Being a natural blood
thinner makes me a great asset to a
diabetic."

"I'm Jim-Niacin, and I
recommend my maintenance dose of
250 mg. of niacin once per day for
one not showing any diabetic
symptoms. On the other hand, for
anyone experiencing the symptoms of
diabetes, especially numbness in the
lower extremities I recommend my
unclogging dose of 250 mg. of niacin
twice per day.

"Too high of a dose of niacin can
cause liver damage and high blood
sugar levels, but too low of a dose
does no good. The 500 mg.
maximum dose per day seems to be
just enough to be effective.

"There have been many lower
extremities cut off because of
diabetes, but I truly believe that if
they had only given Jim-Niacin a
chance I would have saved some of
those limbs."

"Is there anyone else?" said B-
12. "There it is folks, three powerful
weapons to deal with this scourge

diabetes. Now, for the final question
of the evening, the question is what
can we do to prevent extremely dry
skin?"

"I'm Gina-Evening Primrose Oil,
I'm an essential fatty acid and I'm one
of the good oils that the body needs
for beautiful skin. I recommend 1000-
3000 mg. of evening primrose oil per
day."

"I'm Jim-Niacin. In my view
problems with dry skin, toe nail
funguses, dandruff, and other skin
problems is almost always a problem
with blood circulation especially in the
capillaries and small blood vessels.

"For extremely dry skin I
recommend my unclogging dose of
250 mg. twice per day after a meal
until the extremely dry skin condition
has been cured, then throttle down to
250 mg. once a day for maintenance.
But, be aware, most humans fear me,
and for good reason, because my
doses are no Sunday picnic or stroll
through the park. My doses may
heat up your skin like it is on fire and
turn it as red as a beet.

"This flushing process is
unpredictable, sometimes it will not

happen at all, then other times it will last anywhere from five minutes to thirty minutes. It may not be pleasant, but it is my only way of unclogging the capillaries and small blood vessels," said Jim-Niacin.

"Is there anyone else?" said B-12. "What more could one ask for; those were two of the most powerful remedies that I ever heard of in dealing with a pesky humiliating dry skin condition.

"Remember, a dry skin problem is not something to be taken lightly, because you can see what is happening to the outer skin, but what's taking place inside with the vital organs could be a lot worse. "Citizens of Health-land Kingdom, that will end our town hall meeting for tonight, I would like to thank everyone for coming. Have a safe drive home," he said.

Chapter 6

Captain Fredrico was very impressed with the town hall meeting, especially learning how to deal with his long time dry skin problem and toe nail fungus. It had got to the point that he hated to take a shower.

It was bad enough struggling
through the warmer months of the
year, but the approach of winter was
almost terrifying because a dry skin
problem becomes much worse during
the winter months. Much of the time
during the winter he had to resort to
what is called a bird bath by washing
only his arm pits and private area.
He had tried all kinds of oils, both
internal and external. He had
traveled on the super MD highway to
the cure all metropolis, but all to no
avail. Since the town hall meeting he
had started off on Jim-Niacin's
unclogging dose of 250 mg. of niacin
twice a day after a meal.

The resulting benefits were
obvious within a couple of days.
Within days the treatment was so
effective that the captain could barely
wait to jump into the shower for the
slightest reason. Also, within days
his toe nails had started clearing and
should be completely clear within a
few months.

Also, in a few months the
mayoral election will be taking place.
Captain Fredrico felt very good about
his chances of winning. According

to the latest poll he had a four point
lead.

That night as he and Jan were
setting in the den watching TV,
Captain Fredrico said, "You know,
Jan, if I do become mayor of Health-
land Kingdom I'm going to recognize
Jim-Niacin by declaring a Jim-Niacin
day."

"I know, dear, how much you
love Jim-Niacin. He made it possible
for you to be able to take regular
showers again without you having to
lotion down almost your whole body."
"I don't care how much he is
feared and misunderstood," said the
Captain. "As far as I'm concerned
Jim-Niacin is a miracle vitamin."

"I agree, my darling husband,
about Jim-Niacin's abilities, if humans
would just give him a chance he
would save most of the lower
extremities that are being lost
because of Mr. Diabetes Disease."

The Captain got up from his
recliner, walked over to Jan and gave
her a warm tender kiss on her waiting
luscious lips and said, "I'm off to bed,
dear, I'll wait up for you."
"I won't be long, dear," said Jan.

Is Immigration A Blessing In Disguise?

Things had been rather calm in Health-land Kingdom for the last few months VC, VE, and John-pyridoxine all were very busy taking care of the town's population. About the only thing going on was the mayoral election coming up very soon.

They all thought the town hall meeting did a lot of good for the community. They felt it educated the citizens that there was a lot they could do for themselves concerning their health care.

That means that one will not have   to jump on the super MD highway for the slightest little pin prick or minor inconvenience. Sure, there is only so much we vitamins, minerals, herbs, etc. can do to promote health, we don't try to be everything to everybody.
After the town hall meeting Mr.

Disease was steaming mad. He was even thinking of calling a meeting of all the different diseases. The nerve of those vitamins, minerals, humans, herbs and other nutrients trying to get

together and put him and his friends
out of business.

They want to try to put his most
successful friends like cancer,
diabetes, heart disease, and AIDS
out of business. He was not having
it; that was not going to be tolerated.
Mr. Disease started planning.

He would try to attack their left flank
by bringing back some of his old
friends like the Black Plague,
Tuberculosis, and West Nile, next he
would try to rush their right flank with
AIDS to try to split their force, then he
would try to rout them up the middle
with lots of Cancer and Heart
Disease.

I will take no prisoners. Who do
they think this is, this is Mr. Disease
and I don't play, I even quit school
because they had recess. It is on.
How dare they have this town hall
meeting to try and get rid of me and
my friends.

After a long hot summer the day
of the mayoral election had finally
arrived and it looked like it was going
to be a big turn out. At seven o'clock
p.m. Captain Fredrico, Jan, Bob, and
Melinda had comfortable seats at

election headquarters. All of the
election precincts closed at seven
o'clock p.m. sharp.

The captain and his family
started   watching the tally on the
big electronic board as the precincts
came in. Captain Fredrico jumped
out to an early four point lead and
was able to maintain the lead
throughout the night as the precincts
came in. Then, finally the election
supervisor announced, "Citizens of
Health-land Kingdom the mayor elect
is Orry Fredrico." Within seconds
several microphones were thrust in
Captain Fredrico's face.

A reporter was almost yelling,
"Captain Fredrico, how does it feel
being the mayor elect of Health-land
Kingdom."

"First, I would like to thank my
family and all of the volunteers that
worked so hard on my behalf to make
this   happen. Next, I would like to
thank all of the citizens of Health-land
Kingdom who had the faith and trust
in me and backed it up by turning out
to vote for me.

"Also, I would like to inform those
that did not vote for me that I will be

mayor of all the citizens of Health-
land Kingdom. Finally, I would like to
thank my opponent for a good clean
hard fought campaign. Thanks again
everyone. Good night."

Chapter 7

About one month after Captain
Fredrico had been sworn in as mayor
of Health-land Kingdom, he
announced that the first Saturday in
March would be recognized by the
town as Jim-Niacin's day.

On the morning of the first
Saturday in March Mayor Fredrico
stood at the podium at Healthy living
park before a very large crowd.

"Citizens of Health-land
Kingdom, today as your mayor I am
proclaiming today as Jim-Niacin's
day. We have on hand plenty of free
food, drinks, and entertainment. To
kick off this festive day, I'm going to
deliver this short speech about the
vitamin citizen we are celebrating
today.

"Citizens of Health-land, Jim-
Niacin is sort of an enigma. Many
here had never heard of him, and of

those that had, many of them fear
and hate him. Still there is a great
many that love this vitamin to death.

"I myself am one of those that
dearly love Jim-Niacin and the good
work he does. I am not telling you
what I heard about Jim-Niacin, I'm
telling you what I've personally
experienced with my dealing with Jim-
Niacin. I'm giving it to you first hand,
straight from the horse's mouth.

"As I've told my wife and many
others, I don't care what anyone
says, to me Jim-Niacin is a miracle
vitamin. This small, quiet, lowly
member of the powerful B vitamin
family is a Godsend as far as I'm
concerned. As a proud virile human
male I think of the many, many years
that I suffered with extremely dry
skin.

"For years I tried everything to
get relief from this annoying dry skin
condition. Even at the cure all
metropolis they just prescribed an
extremely expensive body cream that
did little better than cheap over-the-
counter lotions.

"Bathing and warm water had
become the enemy. Washing only

arm pits and the private area was
becoming the norm, and I just hated
my predicament. To me cleanliness
is next to   Godliness.

"Sure, I had heard of Jim-Niacin,
but it was mainly bad stuff, I never
knew about his real power until I
attended the town hall meeting. Over
the years the dry skin problem was
getting worse. Some type of fungus
had invaded my toe nails and my skin
was losing its luster in a few
locations.

"The battle for healthy skin was a
battle I knew I was losing , but no one
could help me and I didn't know what
to do. All of my life I've never been a
quitter, I knew there was an answer,
the problem was finding it, so I just
kept on searching and searching.

"I was at my wits end, nothing or
no one seemed able to help me find
relief from my extremely dry skin
condition. Then, at the final hour
when all seemed lost and there was
no hope left, Jim-Niacin came riding
in on a big white horse at the town
hall meeting.

"At the town hall meeting Jim-
Niacin gave out his unclogging dose

of 250 mg. twice a day after a meal.
The first thing is I must warn you that
taking Jim-Niacin's unclogging dose is
no cake walk or stroll through the
park. That is the reason many who
have tried taking Jim's doses don't
like him and is afraid of him.

"When Jim goes to work
unclogging those capillaries and small
blood vessels it is not pleasant by any
means. This flushing process varies
in intensity, sometimes it may be
mild, then at other times your skin
may feel like it is literally on fire.

"This flushing process may last
anywhere from five to thirty minutes,
but seldom lasts more than thirty
minutes. I have no evidence to
support this, but I believe diabetes
itself is caused by a deficiency in
niacin, chromium, and a few other
nutrients.

"Citizens of Health-land I could
go on and on praising Jim-Niacin
because in the past he truly has been
an unsung hero. I will add this and
come to a close. Don't ever go over
his maximum 500 mg. daily dose or it
could cause liver damage.

"In closing, I will assure you that

his unclogging dose got rid of my
dandruff, dry skin, toe nail fungus,
etc. Stand up Jim-Niacin and say a
few words," concluded Captain
Fredrico.

As Jim-Niacin arrived at the
podium he stood tall and proud.
The audience went wild with
applause, then chanted, "We love you
Jim, we love you Jim, we love you
"Thank you, thank you, thank
you," said Jim-Niacin, "and may God
bless this great town and keep it
healthy always."

THE END

Freddie L Sirmans, Sr.
Website: www.FLSirmans.com

www.ingramcontent.com/pod-product-compliance
Lightning Source LLC
Chambersburg PA
CBHW051322170526
45166CB00002B/643

* 9 7 8 1 5 0 0 3 0 9 8 2 4 *